D1581648

Prevention is Better Than Cure

LEARNING FROM ADVERSE EVENTS IN HEALTHCARE

Prevention is Better Than Cure

LEARNING FROM ADVERSE EVENTS IN HEALTHCARE

Ian Leistikow MD, PhD

Senior Inspector
Dutch Healthcare Inspectorate

and

Researcher
Institute of Health Policy & Management
Erasmus University Rotterdam
The Netherlands

CRC Press
Taylor & Francis Group
Boca Raton London New York

CRC Press is an imprint of the
Taylor & Francis Group, an **informa** business

CRC Press
Taylor & Francis Group
6000 Broken Sound Parkway NW, Suite 300
Boca Raton, FL 33487-2742

© 2017 by Taylor & Francis Group, LLC
CRC Press is an imprint of Taylor & Francis Group, an Informa business

Library of Congress Cataloging-in-Publication Data

Names: Leistikow, Ian, author.
Title: Prevention is better than cure / Ian Leistikow.
Other titles: Voorkomen is beter. English
Description: Boca Raton, FL : CRC Press, 2017.
Identifiers: LCCN 2016035053| ISBN 9781138197763 (pbk. : alk. paper) | ISBN
9781315276366 (ebook)
Subjects: | MESH: Medical Errors--prevention & control | Patient
Harm--prevention & control | Case Reports
Classification: LCC R729.8 | NLM WB 100 | DDC 610.289--dc23
LC record available at https://lccn.loc.gov/2016035053

Visit the Taylor & Francis Web site at http://www.taylorandfrancis.com

and the CRC Press Web site at http://www.crcpress.com

Contents

Preface

Why do things go wrong in healthcare? Every country, every culture, has a form of healthcare set up to protect fellow humans against discomfort, disability, disease and death. Nevertheless, this same system, in all countries and cultures, is regularly the *cause* of discomfort, disability, disease and death.

Prevention is Better than Cure describes real-life cases of serious adverse events in healthcare and reflects on the underlying causes. These are eye-openers to many healthcare professionals, because most are still not trained in safety competencies. Due to this, they are unaware how circumstances influence their behaviour and how this behaviour can impair patient safety. Not reading a patient's chart, neglecting concerns raised by nursing, assuming something has been taken care of without making sure, letting relationship issues trump safety issues, accepting exhausting working hours, are just a few examples. A challenge within healthcare is to engage in a dialogue about behaviour without regressing to 'blaming and shaming'.

Prevention is Better than Cure contributes to making unsafe behaviour something one can talk about non-judgementally. It offers healthcare professionals concrete suggestions on how they can avoid adverse events and further improve the quality of the care they deliver.

Ian Leistikow

About the author

Ian Leistikow is a non-practising physician. He was the coordinator of the patient safety programme within the University Medical Centre Utrecht, the Netherlands, from 2003 to 2011. This programme comprised, for example, the introduction of Root Cause Analysis (RCA), proactive risk analysis (HFMEA), research on handoffs, research on patient participation and a video game on patient safety (www.airmedicsky1.org). He has set up various patient safety-related training modules, has published multiple articles about patient safety and is co-author of a book on RCA. In December 2011 he published his PhD thesis on how the Board of Directors can lead patient safety improvements. His thesis is condensed into an article that was published in the *BMJ* in July 2011. In 2014 he published a Dutch book on learning from Sentinel Events, which was widely recognised in the Netherlands. Since April 2011 Ian has worked as Senior Inspector at the Dutch Healthcare Inspectorate. There his tasks include judging the quality of sentinel event analysis reports from hospitals and coordinating the Dutch national set of quality indicators for hospitals. Ian is member of the Strategic Advisory Board of the International Forum on Quality and Safety in Healthcare. He is also one of the initiators of GetUpGetBetter (www.getupgetbetter.com), a series of international healthcare quality competitions, that is currently being developed.

Abbreviations

A&E	Accident and Emergency
ADCA	autosomal dominant cerebellar ataxia
APACHE	Acute Physiology and Chronic Health Evaluation
CRM	crew resource management
CRP	C-reactive protein
CT	computed tomography
CTG	cardiotocography
CTS	carpal tunnel syndrome
CVC	central venous catheter
DNA	deoxyribonucleic acid
ECG	electrocardiogram
ENT	ear/nose/throat
FBS	fetal scalp blood sampling
FFP	fresh frozen plasma
FHM	familial hemiplegic migraine
fMRI	functional magnetic resonance imaging
GP	general practitioner
HRO	High Reliability Organisation
ICU	Intensive Care Unit
IV	intravenous
MRI	magnetic resonance imaging
NSTEMI	non-ST segment elevation myocardial infarction
ORS	oral rehydration supplement
RCA	Root Cause Analysis
RRS	rapid response system
UMC	University Medical Centre

Introduction

EVERY DAY PATIENTS DIE AS A RESULT OF ERRORS IN HEALTHCARE

Why do things go wrong in healthcare? Why do fathers, mothers, grandparents, children, loved ones die as result of a system that was designed to make them better? Every country, every culture, has a form of healthcare. This is set up to protect fellow humans against discomfort, disability, disease and death. Nevertheless, this same system, in all countries and cultures, is regularly the cause of discomfort, disability, disease and death. In my country, the Netherlands, research showed that 1.6% of patients admitted to hospitals in 2011/2012 suffered a form of potentially preventable harm[1]. That amounts to 70 patients each day, of whom 2–3 die as a result of the preventable harm. Every day, day in day out. And these are only the hospitalised patients. We have no insight into the measure of preventable harm in mental health, elderly care, home care or primary care. All countries that have performed similar studies, found similar results. It's staggering. Since I became involved in Patient Safety, I have seen thousands of examples of harm caused by healthcare delivery. From events with relatively little harm, to heart breaking tragedies. First, as a member of the incident reporting committee of the University Medical Centre Utrecht (UMC Utrecht). This committee reviews all reported adverse events, which amounted to about 600 a year when I joined in 2003 and increased to around 3000 annually when I left to work for the Dutch Healthcare Inspectorate, my current job, in 2011. At the Inspectorate I joined the team that assesses all sentinel events reported by hospitals (adverse events that lead to serious harm or death) and the analyses hospitals perform in the wake of these events[2]. In this capacity I see around 800 sentinel events annually.

FROM FIXING THE BLAME TO FIXING THE SYSTEM

In 2003 I became involved in setting up the patient safety programme within the UMC Utrecht. We started from scratch – the Dutch word for patient safety at that time literally did not exist. One of the first themes we picked up was incident analysis and the UMC Utrecht became the first hospital in the Netherlands to implement Root Cause Analysis (RCA) within the whole hospital. We discovered that systematic investigation of adverse events led to a much better understanding of the root causes of unintended outcomes. It made us look at the system as a whole, instead of just focussing on the individuals who had made mistakes somewhere along the line. With 'system' I mean the tasks, technology, organisation and environment the individual performs in[3]. In most cases, the mistakes people make would be made by others too, given similar circumstances. It turned out to be much more useful to redesign the work environment than to punish individuals or to tell them to pay more attention next time. 'Why don't the nurses just read the ampoule?' became 'How can we improve the readability of the ampoules?' Our focus shifted from fixing the blame to fixing the system. At the time this was ground breaking.

THERE IS A THIRST FOR KNOWLEDGE ON HOW TO PREVENT ADVERSE EVENTS

In my current role, I am regularly asked why we don't share our database of adverse events with the hospitals, to share the learning. This has even become a public debate in the Netherlands in 2016. Sometimes it's possible, when specific themes emerge from the reports we receive. An example of such a theme is serious harm to infants after anaesthesia, which was independently reported by different hospitals. Another example is recurrent reports of diagnoses found by radiologists but missed by the doctors treating the patient. In these cases the Inspectorate informed the relevant medical societies (the Dutch Society of Anaesthesia, the Dutch Society of Radiology) and requested them to work on decreasing these problems. But an overview, or a 'top 10', of reported adverse events is difficult to produce in such a way that healthcare providers, professionals and patients can actually use this information to reduce harm. This is an internationally recognised problem. Many countries have established incident reporting systems, but the value of these systems is increasingly subject to debate[4,5]. Reporting systems, both local and national, are overwhelmed by the volume of reports and fall short in defining recommendations for improving healthcare safety: "We collect too much and do too little."[6] This is an enormous challenge around the globe. But while we are thinking about how best to meet this challenge, healthcare continues and mistakes are being made that could have been avoided if lessons from previous similar mistakes had been shared.

LESSONS THAT WOULD HAVE BEEN USEFUL FOR ME AS CLINICIAN

This is the reason why I wrote this book. I felt an obligation to share the information that I had gathered over the years, to mould this into practical lessons that can help healthcare professionals and patients reduce the chances of becoming involved in an adverse event. I wanted to produce something that would have helped me, if I were still a clinician. I wanted to make it generic so it would be applicable throughout the various healthcare fields. But, at the same time, I wanted to keep the lessons simple, pint-sized, so they fall within the circle of influence of the reader, whatever his or her position within the healthcare system. That led me to the subject of 'behaviour'.

UNSAFE BEHAVIOUR IS OFTEN UNINTENDED

When we learned how system failures enable adverse events and how to improve system safety, we also discovered that safe systems are no match for unsafe behaviour: not reading a patient's chart, neglecting concerns raised by nursing, delegating tasks to juniors who lack essential experience, assuming something has been taken care of without making sure, letting relationship issues trump safety issues, downplaying or hiding mistakes, accepting exhausting working hours, to name just a few. This is the kind of behaviour that an outsider, a patient, will judge as unacceptable and reprehensible, especially when an adverse outcome becomes apparent and a causal relationship between the behaviour and the outcome is inferred.

However, this judgement in hindsight is often not shared by the individual who expressed the behaviour. In many cases, the behaviour results from a trade-off between, for example, safety and efficiency. It seems more efficient not to come to the hospital for every query a junior pages you for. It costs valuable time to sift through the chart of every routine patient. Even more often, the person is not aware of his or her own behaviour, let alone of the possible consequences this behaviour can have on safety. It never comes to mind that a conflict with a colleague could lead to unsafe care. For an outsider with modest knowledge of safety management, the ignorance within the healthcare community pertaining to safety can be baffling. But healthcare professionals have never been trained in safety. Most of us are unconsciously incompetent. During my 6 years of medical training I was never once told that I would make mistakes as doctor, let alone how to prevent these mistakes. Not how to handle my own mistakes, nor how to handle colleagues who made mistakes. I was taught how to break bad news to a patient ("I'm sorry Mrs Jones, you have cancer"), but never how to break bad news that I was part of ("I'm sorry Mrs Jones, you have cancer and you could have had more treatment options if I had not missed this abnormality on your X-ray last year"). It was simply not part of the medical curriculum. The message was implicit but crystal clear: if you make a mistake, it's your own stupid fault.

BEHAVIOUR DETERMINES SAFETY

Until the year 2000 'blaming and shaming' was the norm within healthcare when something went wrong. The 1999 report *To Err is Human* by the Institute of Medicine made a major contribution to translating the importance of systems thinking from other industries to healthcare[7]. This led to a shift in focus from human failure to system failure. In my country this new way of thinking gained attention around 2004 but it took several more years before it became widely accepted. After some years of experience with this new paradigm, people started to run into the limitations of putting systems theory into practice. An important limitation was that it offered no tools to handle behavioural issues. There was not much one could do about an authoritative doctor who refused to abide by certain protocols, but who had not been involved in any visible adverse outcome. The challenge we face today is to engage in a dialogue about behaviour without falling back into the 'blame and shame' era. To see behaviour as both an individual choice and as a result of the systems around this individual.

Behaviour is a choice, but is it also influenced by contextual factors. I behave differently in a job interview than in a bar with my mates. In the end, behaviour determines safety, inside and outside of healthcare. Now that we have started to achieve some control over the system, behaviour is becoming the weakest link. I'm not talking about extreme behaviour, but about the everyday behaviour that expresses unconscious incompetence in basic safety management. I am convinced that changing this behaviour is the next step we must take to improve further healthcare quality and safety.

WORKING ON PATIENT SAFETY HAS CHANGED ME

I am very grateful for having had the opportunity to learn so much since 2003 about safety in general, and patient safety specifically. Over the years I have had the honour to meet and collaborate with numerous gifted, inspirational and wise people from around the globe. Sharing thoughts and experiences on how to improve healthcare has also had a profound effect on me. It taught me a lot about how I think and behave. These new insights influence my behaviour on a daily basis: as road user, as healthcare inspector, as husband and certainly as father of two young children. It would also have influenced my behaviour as clinician, had I continued practising. In the adverse event reports that I read, I can see that many clinicians, general practitioners (GPs), dentists, nurses, paramedics and other allied health professionals lack this background and I am convinced healthcare would be a safer place if they had shared my history.

UNSAFE BEHAVIOUR MUST BE DISCUSSED

That is how I came to write this book. I want to share the knowledge and experiences I have been fortunate enough to collect over the years and offer healthcare professionals concrete suggestions on how they can avoid adverse events. I want to create awareness about how circumstances influence behaviour and how this behaviour can impair patient safety. I unequivocally reject the idea that a focus on behaviour implies a return to blaming and shaming. In my opinion, healthcare professionals are not reprehensible if they express the behaviour I describe in this book, because I am convinced the large majority are not aware of their own behaviour or the consequences behaviour can have, just like I wasn't. And even now that I am aware, I still catch myself acting unsafely all too often. It's probably impossible to get it right every time, but it's certainly possible to get better at it. With this book I want to contribute to making unsafe behaviour something we can talk about non-judgementally, suggest alternatives and convince healthcare professionals that these can help to further improve the quality of the care they deliver.

OUTLINE OF THE BOOK

Each chapter starts with a true case story. Each case has been written in the first-person from the perspective of one of the involved actors: the doctor, nurse, patient or family of the patient. In the second part of the chapter I reflect on the case by highlighting one or two elements from the case that offer learning opportunities. I end each chapter with a concrete suggestion for doctors (or other healthcare professionals) on what they can do to reduce the chance of becoming involved in a similar adverse event and how they can engage the patient in this.

I do not claim to possess the 'absolute truth' and my reflections are open for debate. It would be wonderful if readers engage in discussions with each other and reformulate my recommendations to fit better within their own culture or working environment.

A FEW DISCLOSURE ISSUES UP FRONT

All cases are based on real life situations, but none of the cases is a literal description of one single case. I have drawn from several situations, have changed certain details and added others, so as to prevent recognisability for the people involved. The character descriptions and dialogues are made up. In this way I tried to create realistic descriptions of cases without breaching the privacy of those involved.

I have written this book in a private capacity. The views expressed and the recommendations are those of the author and do not necessarily reflect official positions of the Dutch Healthcare Inspectorate.

I have tried to back my reflections with scientific literature, but I do not claim this book is scientific.

I also do not claim this book offers a complete overview. There are many more ways to improve the quality and safety of healthcare. It is not a 'top 10' causes of adverse events. It is, however, a book I wish I had read during my own medical training. It would have made me a better doctor.

IMPROVING WITHOUT INQUISITIONS

Let me end by emphasising that the quality of healthcare in most nations is excellent. That said, every adverse event is one too many. Many of the cases in this book are dramatic. They were tragic for the patient, the family and the caregivers involved. Some scars will never heal. I don't want to come across as melodramatic, I want to draw a realistic picture of what happens in healthcare. It is my conviction that we, patients, professionals and public, can collaborate to make healthcare even better than it is already. For this we will first need to face the current situation, with an open mind, not judgementally. If we are truly willing to learn, we can achieve so much more. I hope this book can in some way help the reader contribute to this goal.

CHAPTER 1
Worst case scenario

THE CASE

I had been an ophthalmologist for 15 years, the previous 13 years as a consultant at this hospital, when it happened. A terrible complication, one that I just had not anticipated. But let me start at the beginning.

Sunday, June 15th. Frank Templeman, a healthy 33-year-old sporting enthusiast, is involved in a sailing accident. In an unfortunate crash jibe, the boom smashes into his face fracturing his right cheekbone. In the subsequent fall he also breaks his left wrist.

His sailing buddy brings Frank to the A&E Department of my hospital. His wife and 5-year-old son arrive an hour later, just in time to see him being admitted into the maxillofacial surgery department. I know Frank's family. Some years ago, I would go sailing regularly with Bobby Templeman, Frank's uncle, on his 23-foot Parker off the coast by Emsworth. But on that Sunday afternoon I did not yet know that Frank had been admitted to my hospital. I was not involved in his care until the following Wednesday.

My colleague, Peter Plover, a seasoned oral maxillofacial surgeon, is on call that Sunday. He comes in from home immediately on receiving the call from the A&E department. A trauma surgeon is already busy assessing Frank and has set in motion preparations for a CT scan to be made of his head and cervical spine. Fortunately, no damage is found to the spine. However, the CT scan shows a fracture of the right zygoma continuing through into the base of the orbit. Peter Plover decides to operate immediately on account of the risk the fracture poses for the right eye. During the same session the trauma surgeon also treats the broken wrist.

We see a zygoma fracture about every week, our hospital being located in a small coastal town with more than its fair share of night-time brawls. So this treatment has become quite routine for us. The oral maxillofacial surgeons generally don't consult an ophthalmologist unless they suspect an injury to the eye. With Frank Templeman this was not the case. The boom had hit his cheekbone and seemed to have missed his eye.

1

Both procedures are carried out successfully on the Sunday evening following the accident. The next day, a nurse reports that Frank has diplopia, double vision. Doctor Simon Everhouse, a colleague of Peter Plover, examines Frank. The left eye is fine. The right eye is difficult to examine due to the swollen bruising beneath the eye. Simon can't get a good reading on the pupillary light reflex. He orders another CT scan and evaluates the scan himself. He rules out damage to the ophthalmic nerve, sees no signs of haemorrhage within the orbit and confirms that the zygoma has been adequately aligned.

On Wednesday Peter Plover consults me. Frank had complained about blurred vision. That afternoon is the first time I see Frank since his admission to the hospital. I introduce myself and inquire if he is related to Bobby Templeman. He tells me he is and we chat about sailing while I examine him. His right eye is swollen, but not more than could be expected after a surgical procedure on a fractured zygoma. The contusion makes it hard to close the eye completely. I suspect that incomplete closure of the eye has dried the eye causing the blurred vision. I instruct the nurse to bandage the eye. Later that day Peter Plover conducts his ward rounds and orders a skull X-ray to check the orbit. The photo shows nothing worrying.

However, on Thursday, when the nurse changes the bandage, Frank discovers he can hardly see with his right eye. By the time I arrive on the ward, a distressed Frank exclaims: "I can't see!" In a split second the differential diagnosis shoots through my head: occlusion of the retinal artery, compressive optic neuropathy, retinal detachment, papilloedema, glaucoma, hyphaema, corneal abrasion... I begin a full examination of the eye with my ophthalmoscope and discover the problem: retinal detachment. I immediately call surgery to set up an emergency procedure the same day, but unfortunately it turns out to be too late to restore his vision. Frank's right eye will remain impaired for life.

Naturally, we went over this case extensively. The oral maxillofacial surgeons had examined the eye but had not seen signs of any external trauma. In hindsight, it seems probable that the boom had hit the eye after all and that the force of the blow had torn the retina. In the days following, the retina had slowly started to detach itself, until on Wednesday the detachment had reached the macula and caused the blurred vision. Had I only examined the eye with my ophthalmoscope that day, I would have seen it and maybe, just maybe, we could have prevented further harm. We can only guess. It's impossible to prove that we could have saved his vision. None of my colleagues at the hospital had experienced a similar case before. We, therefore, concluded that it was a tragic and extremely rare complication. And, for us, that was the end of it.

REFLECTION

Is there no other conclusion that we can draw from the case of Frank Templeman other than that this was an unfortunate, but rare, complication that could not have been avoided? If so, then this would lead logically to the consequent conclusion that nothing could be changed to decrease the chance of recurrence in the future. As the physicians involved in Frank's care also concluded: it was unavoidable so there is nothing to improve. Case closed.

But, what if one sees the adverse event as not having diagnosed the retinal detachment earlier, rather than as the retinal detachment itself? That offers a different perspective on the case which could lead to a different conclusion....

The patient had complained he had double vision the day after the surgery. The surgeon had, therefore, tried to examine the eye and assess the pupillary light reflex. But he could not perform this diagnostic adequately due to the swollen bruising around the eye. He then ordered a CT scan. The scan did not show bleeding behind the eye, so the eye was not being pushed out of its socket, which could have explained the symptoms. The optical nerve and the bone structures appeared to be fine. The surgeon was reassured. This was the first moment in which the underlying pathology of the eye was missed. The surgeon tried to assess the pupillary reflex, but failed to do so. You often find in the reconstruction of adverse events in healthcare that a doctor tried to undertake an examination of some sort. Having failed to perform it adequately, for whatever reason, he or she let it go instead of pursuing the line of thought and taking action to obtain adequate diagnostics.

A fetal monitor pattern that is difficult to assess, a blurred X-ray, an insufficient amount of tissue for pathology, confusing anamnestic information. These are all situations where, for whatever reason, the doctor can give up and the information missed turns out to be pivotal as events unfold further. I assume that the oral maxillofacial surgeon Peter Plover had a reason why he tried to assess the pupillary reflex. He must have had a hunch of sorts, otherwise he would not have tried. But when he couldn't get it done, he did not persevere. He did not consult a colleague or an ophthalmologist in order to perform the diagnostics properly. He did order a CT scan and let the result reassure him. However, you cannot assess a pupillary reflex on a CT scan. So he did not persevere to find out if the patient's pupillary reflex was indeed intact. The story does not give us any clue as to why he was not more persistent. We will never know whether the patient's pupillary reflex was intact at that time. But what we do know is that if the surgeon had consulted an ophthalmologist who had then examined the eye properly, the tear in the retina would have been discovered. Action could then have been taken to prevent further harm to the eye. By not following through on his own hunch, the surgeon deprived the patient of the chance of a timely recovery.

Once you know the outcome, it is easy to judge the events leading to that adverse outcome. Should the surgeon not have done A? Why didn't the nurse just do B?, etc. This is called 'hindsight bias': in hindsight the adverse outcome seems to be predictable and the behaviour of the people involved is judged as inadequate. Surgeon Peter Plover did not know on Monday that his patient would lose the sight of his right eye by Thursday, otherwise he would have acted differently that week.

In the courses on incident analysis in which I participated as trainer, we always emphasised the danger of hindsight bias. As investigators we easily confuse our reality with the reality of the people we investigate[1]. We argue that you should not judge someone's actions on the outcome, but always on the circumstances and the information available at the time of the action. What could he have done better at that moment in time, with the available knowledge, or why was essential knowledge not available at that time? This is incredibly difficult for humans to do, because we have been programmed from our childhood to base our judgement on the outcome. In 2002, Harvard researchers showed fictional case reports of adverse healthcare events to a group of doctors and a group of people not working in healthcare, in other words the general public[2]. They had made two versions of each case, one where the patient suffers serious harm and one where the patient escapes harm. Each respondent received one of the versions and was asked to answer a series of questions regarding responsibility and accountability, such as 'should the hospital/doctor/nurse be sued?'. Respondents who read the case reports with the adverse outcome were significantly more prone to punishing the healthcare providers involved than those respondents who read the identical cases without a serious outcome. This was the case for both the doctors and the public. This is a striking example of how hindsight bias affects our judgement.

In my daily work as a healthcare inspector, I am always very wary of hindsight bias, both in my own reasoning and in the reasoning within the adverse event analysis reports that I read. My team never accepts human failure as a root cause. 'The nurse did not follow protocol', or 'the doctor did not pursue his line of inquiry' are not root causes. There is always a reason why they acted as they did. Understanding the reason why can give a lead as to what the organisation can do to decrease the chance of similar adverse events occurring. In the case of Frank Templeman, the oral maxillofacial surgeon knew that the patient had double vision. He knew that this problem would not be solved by a CT scan. Neither did the CT scan provide him with an answer as to why the patient had double vision. Given that he wanted to test the pupillary light reflex, it is safe to assume that the surgeon considered problems with the optic nerve as a possible cause. Why did he not pursue this line of thought? Why did he not consult a colleague or an ophthalmologist? The failure to identify a cause for the double vision should have set alarm bells ringing, not reassured him. It's not clear what diagnosis the surgeon had in mind for the double vision, nor what he had instructed the nurses to do with regard to following up on the patient's complaint. The information we have suggests that the surgeon could have done more to pursue the cause of the double vision. Double vision is not caused by retinal detachment, but pursuing its cause would have led to earlier detection of the retinal detachment.

Two days later the patient complained about blurred vision. Only then was an ophthalmologist consulted. The ophthalmologist saw a swollen eye that could not be closed. To him it seemed logical that this caused the blurred vision and so he instructed the nurse to apply a protective bandage. The ophthalmologist did not do a comprehensive examination of the eye. It was not until the next day, Thursday, after the patient complained of being blind in one eye that he used his ophthalmoscope. With my basic ophthalmological knowledge, I can understand that a dry eye is on top of the list of possible causes for blurred vision when the eye cannot close fully. And, of course, the ophthalmologist did not know on

Wednesday that he would discover retinal detachment the next day. But he did know that the patient had had severe trauma of his cheekbone with a fracture in the base of the eye socket, that he had blurred vision and that impending blindness is always the 'worst case scenario' for a patient with decreasing vision. So why did he not perform a full ocular examination? Just as with the surgeon on Monday, he had let himself be incorrectly reassured without further investigation, without ruling out the 'worst case scenario'.

To me, this is the main lesson from the case of Frank Templeman. The doctors did not put in enough effort to rule out the worst case scenario. We can see this in the case itself and also in the way they evaluated the case afterwards. In the case they did not rule out sufficiently the possibility that the patient was losing his eyesight. In the evaluation they did not rule out sufficiently the possibility that their own actions could have played a role in the delayed discovery of the diagnosis. I can agree with the conclusion that they could not find ways to decrease the chance of retinal detachment as the pathophysiological cause is outside of their remit and ability to control. But there certainly is a prospect for improvement in looking at the organisational cause: not being sufficiently alert to the possible loss of vision.

A medical complication always consists of two elements: a pathophysiological and an organisational one. In other words, the occurrence of the complication and its subsequent detection. Examples include: the anastomotic leak after gastrointestinal surgery and the detection of the leak; delirium and recognising the delirium; spinal fracture and detection of the spinal fracture. In evaluating the case, surgeon Peter Plover, his colleagues and the ophthalmologist only looked at the pathophysiological element and concluded that they could not have prevented the loss of vision. Had they also taken the organisational element into account, they could have drawn a different conclusion. Then they could have concluded that in future situations where a patient complains about loss of vision, they must continue searching until they find the cause. They must rule out the possibility that the patient is progressively losing his or her eyesight. Considering the organisational perspective would have given the team ideas for improvement measures to decrease the chance of blindness for future patients. In other words, to rule out the worst case scenario. This way, the lessons from the Templeman case would have been more widely applicable than just for loss of vision.

Within healthcare there are many examples of spectacular improvements reached through looking at the organisational element of a medical complication. Nowadays, this leads to much larger improvements in outcomes than medical-technical innovations. A 50% reduction in perioperative mortality had never been reached through improving techniques or equipment, but became possible by the organisational intervention of the safe surgery checklist[3,4]. A certain percentage of central line-associated bloodstream infections were always deemed an unavoidable complication, until the American anaesthesiologist Peter Pronovost proved they can be decreased to 0% through organisational improvements[5]. We will always create complications in healthcare, it comes with the territory, but we have an obligation to our patients to do everything in our power to reduce the chance and the consequences. And 'everything' is more than just improving our medical–technical skills. It includes designing the organisation around these skills in such a way that the chance of detecting complications in time to mitigate their consequences is as large as possible. In this way we keep decreasing the chance of adverse outcomes for our patients. One way of doing so is to keep in mind which complication you definitively do not want to miss, which complication can lead to death or permanent disability, what the 'worst case scenario' is. You then pursue every possible indication pointing to this complication until you can reasonably rule it out.

In the case of Frank Templeman this might not have prevented his retinal detachment, but it would have led to an earlier detection and greater opportunities to mitigate its effect.

HOW CAN THIS HELP ME TODAY?

Always keep the 'worst case scenario' in mind and do not rule this out as long as the patient has symptoms that could fit this scenario.

HOW CAN I INVOLVE MY PATIENTS?

Explain to your patient what the 'worst case scenario' is and which symptoms fit, so that the patient can tell you promptly when these symptoms occur.

CHAPTER 2
Your own observation is flawed

THE CASE

Only people with young children or insomnia can really appreciate a good and full night's rest. Sleep had never been an issue for me, but for 2 years it had become one of those things that could really make my day, something special. So it was with a feeling of grateful surprise that I woke up that morning to the noise of our alarm clock. I looked at my husband and whispered: "Third night in a row." "Shh, don't jinx it," Ron replied, afraid that by saying it aloud we would somehow disturb our toddler's newly found equilibrium.

Ron took Daniel to day-care that morning. After they had gone, I tidied up and left for work. It was a beautiful summer morning: floral scents in the air, playful chirping of birds and a soft morning breeze. Just before stepping into my car to drive to the hospital, I took a deep breath and savoured the moment. This day could not have had a better start.

Friends often ask me, especially since I gave birth to Daniel, if it wasn't tough to work on a paediatric ward. All those poor children, the pain, the heart-breaking sorrow. Of course, I reply, it can be hard sometimes, emotional even, but it can also be wonderfully gratifying. Kids don't realise that they are sick, they don't pity themselves. Kids are pure. Adults are often a totally different story. I can still get worked up thinking about some of the adult patients I nursed during my training. The whining, the complaining, they oozed a feeling of being wronged by life. It seemed to me that men where the worst, they just cannot handle even the smallest of grievances. Often I had to restrain myself from pulling one of them out of their beds and dragging their sorry self to an oncology ward. "So you think you are sick? Really? Look at these patients, this is what really being sick is like!" It was bizarre how 'grownups' lose all sense of initiative once they find themselves in a hospital bed. Nurse, can I have a glass of water? Nurse, would you bring me a vase for these flowers? Nurse, would you blow my nose for me? Well educated, responsible adults would become, I don't know, trapped in their own self-pity somehow. Like they had switched themselves off. Anyway, my grades were not

7

very high on these wards. "Irene, you lack empathy," my supervisor would say. I nearly dropped out, until I started my first rounds on a paediatric ward. That was nearly 10 years ago but I can remember it as if it were yesterday. It was like sunshine after a rainy day. I immediately knew this was the place for me, this was where I would thrive. I was very lucky, because I found a job on a paediatric ward right after I qualified. I have worked there since, enjoying it every single day. Kids are great, they don't make a scene out of feeling sick. They are either sick or well, there is nearly nothing in between. And if they don't feel sick, they are happy. Even on a ventilator they can still smile at you. So much strength, so much endurance. I would do anything for my patients.

I changed into my uniform and entered the nurses' office for the handover with plenty of time to spare. The ward was almost fully occupied. There had been an emergency admittance the previous night. A 4-year-old with intussusception; a part of the intestine had invaginated into the adjoining intestinal lumen. It had taken emergency surgery and the parents were, understandably, quite distraught. This had taken up most of the time of my colleagues who had done the night shift. We finished the handover and went to work.

After the ward rounds, I had to flush the central venous line of Tom, a 5-year-old who had undergone major abdominal surgery earlier that week. Tom wasn't doing well, and sadly the doctors doubted that he would survive. Poor Tom had also tested positive for a bacterium that was difficult to treat, so he was nursed in a single room and we had to use protective clothing when taking care of him. Tom had a double lumen catheter that needed to be flushed with heparin twice a day to prevent clotting. This simple task took a lot of trouble because of the extra hygiene measures. But I did it with pleasure. I put on the green cap, facemask and disposable apron, stepped into his room and identified myself. Tom was happy to see me again, despite feeling so sick.

"Hello green monster," he said. "Have you come to eat me?"

"No, unfortunately they won't let us eat the children. We're only allowed to eat crocodiles."

"I don't believe you!"

"Well, have you ever seen a crocodile here?"

"No..."

"Aha, while you figure out why there are no crocodiles here anymore, I will flush your catheter." I opened the drawer of the cabinet. This is where the ampoules of heparin were stored. The drawer had three compartments, one containing ampoules of heparin, one containing ampoules of saline and one with ampoules of water. There were no other ampoules or medication in the room. I took two ampoules of heparin. I swabbed the catheter hub with alcohol and while I waited to let it dry I broke the cap of the first ampoule and drew the fluid up into a syringe. I attached the syringe to the catheter and flushed the line. I took the second ampoule and repeated my actions to flush the second lumen. Directly after I had detached the syringe Tom grabbed my wrist. He shrieked and looked at me with wide, terrified eyes. He was in panic. On the monitor I saw his blood pressure and pulse were rising fast. It took me a second to realise something was seriously wrong. I set off the alarm and tried to console Tom. My colleagues came storming in right at the time Tom's heart stopped. We started resuscitating the boy and after a few minutes the resuscitation team arrived and took over from us. After less than 10 minutes, which felt like hours, Tom's heart was back in action and he was breathing again. The paediatric critical care specialist asked me what had happened and I retrieved the two ampoules from the cabinet. One ampoule read *heparin* and the other ampoule read *adrenaline* (epinephrine). It dawned on me that I had accidently administered adrenaline, instead of heparin. My mind froze, how could this have happened? I could swear I had read the labels of both ampoules before I had drawn them in the syringe...

My team leader was very supportive. She made sure a colleague was called to take over from me that day. We sat in her room where she had brought me a cup of tea. I had been there when the doctor explained to the parents what had gone wrong. The parents were very taken aback, but to my surprise they were not angry with me. Tom's mother even said she was kind of glad that it had been me that made the mistake, because they both knew how committed I was to giving Tom the best possible care. They knew I had not been sloppy. That touched me, but didn't help reduce my feelings of guilt. I kept asking myself how I could have made such a stupid mistake. My colleague Gina entered the team leader's room and sat down. They had reconstructed that there had been a resuscitation in Tom's room some days before Tom had been admitted. During this resuscitation, the team had used adrenaline. One unused ampoule must have been mistakenly placed in the cabinet drawer when they cleaned up. This is how that one ampoule *adrenaline* had snuck itself in between the ampoules of *heparin*. Both ampoules were practically identical: same shape, same white label, a red horizontal line and black letters beneath. That one ampoule should never have been where it was. But for me that was hardly any consolation. I had let Tom down, I should have read the label properly.

REFLECTION

"Why don't they just read?!" was scribbled in the margin of the stack of papers. The professor who had written this, added an extra exclamation mark and drew a thick line beneath the words. It was 2003 and I had just become the new member of the Incident Reporting Committee of the University Medical Centre where I was working. I had a copy of the same stack of papers in front of me where I scribbled my notes on; the patient safety incidents that had been reported the previous week. Every week some of the incidents reported stemmed from misreading medication. Luckily, most often this occurred without serious consequences for the patient. I quickly learned there are myriad ways medication can end up in the wrong dose or in the wrong patient: prescription errors, pharmacy errors (which we seldom saw), errors in preparing the medication on the ward, dosage errors, administration errors, to name a few. That last category included those medication errors that stemmed from a nurse misreading a label. And every time we discussed such an error, one of the members of the committee would groan "Learn to read, dammit." During my first year as member of the committee the discussion was started several times about introducing a form of colour coding to help prevent reading errors. To the clinicians on the team this seemed like a logical safety measure. The pharmacist, however, was against this measure because on the one hand it would be impossible to give all medications a unique colour, and on the other hand this measure would introduce new forms of unsafety because the colour coding would differ between hospitals. If we were to introduce colour coding, this must be done on a national level. And that paralysed the discussion because our committee had no way of influencing national policy. So we were back to square one: the nurse should just read it properly.

Later that year, a friend of mine sent me the email below. It was in the time that internet and email were becoming mainstream and people were sending so-called 'funny emails' to everybody on their address list. Most of these mails were a waste of time, but this one I saved and have used since in over a hundred presentations:

I cluond't bilevee taht I cluod autclaly uednsrtad waht I was rdaenig. Unisg the ilrcndeibe pewor of the hamun biarn, aoccdring to reserach at Cbmairdge Utvinresiy, it dseo'nt mttaer in waht oedrr the ltteres in a wrod aer, the olny iopmtrant tnihg is taht the fsrit and lsat ltteer be in the rhgit pcale. The rset can be a tatol mses and you can raed it whtiuot a pborelm. Tihs is bacesue the hamun mnid deos not raed erevy ltteer by iestfl, but the wrod as a wlohe. Azamnig, hhu? Yaeh and I aawlys tuohhgt slepilng was itopmtran! See if yuor feirdns can raed tihs too!

We don't read every letter by itself, but the word as a whole. Many years later, at a Human Factors course, I was taught how this works. Humans are able to differentiate between signal and noise. If you appreciate the cello, you will be able to detect the sound of the cello among all the other instruments when listing to an orchestra playing. This human characteristic prevents us from drowning in all the stimuli that are constantly flooding us: the purr of computers, tapping on keyboards, conversing colleagues, beeps, alarms, doors closing, lights flashing, smells, temperature... If all these stimuli were registered by us, it would drive us mad. One sign of burn-out is actually the decreased ability to mute useless signals. So it is a healthy and useful property of humans to be able to differentiate between signal and noise and that 'half a word is enough'. This makes it possible for us to read the email text above, even though it is 'mumbo jumbo'. But this same property leads to misinterpretation of signals, such as, as in the case of Tom, misreading. The odds are you will read what you expect to read, if the words are similar. If you expect to read 'heparin' because all the ampoules from that drawer always have this word on their label, you will honestly read 'heparin' even if the label says 'adrenaline'– especially if the letters are in an identical environment (white label, red line, black letters). I could not believe this until I had read the email above. 'Learn to read' is not going to solve this problem, because you read what you expect to read.

This problem has been recognised as a major issue in medication safety and a fitting acronym has been found: SALAD: Sound Alike Look Alike Drugs. Vincristine vinblastine, amiloride amlodipine, clonazepam lorazepam, diprivan ditropan... The Canadian Institute for Safe Medication Practice has published a comprehensive list of examples on its website[1]. Some occur because the names resemble each other, some because the medication looks identical. Pharmaceutical companies sometimes use very similar packaging for very different drugs. One example is a pain medication that had both a box and a strip that looked virtually identical to those of metformin, a drug to control high blood sugar. These are not medications you want to mix up. Another example is when drugs have different doses and these look alike. A case illustrating the possible consequences, which raised a lot of media attention, was the heparin overdose of six babies in Indiana in 2006[2]. A pharmacy technician had loaded the cabinet with heparin at 10,000 units/ml, instead of hep-lock, at 10 units/ml. The nurses did not notice the difference. Three babies died as result. Some pharmacies adjust font size to make the differences between drugs more visible, for example: CLONazepam, LORazepam. This makes it more difficult to misread the label. Another medication safety measure that is used ubiquitously, not just for SALAD, is the double check. One nurse asks another nurse to check if he or she is about to administer the right medication. In practice the double check is often executed wrongly: "10 mil heparin?" one nurse askes another while showing the ampoule. If done this way, the second nurse is tricked into reading what the first nurse expects to be read. Especially as the second nurse often just quickly glances at the ampoule as he or she was focused on another task, so the second nurse is not 100% alert. The proper way to do a double check is to show the ampoule and then ask, "What medication is this, what is the dose, how should I administer this and to which patient?" As you read this, you'll probably feel this is not a realistic way of communicating between professionals. It feels like the nurse is saying "I found this ampoule and I don't have a clue what to do next." Even so, it does actually work better this way because the second nurse is forced to think analytically as supposed to intuitively, if only asked to verify information. I will go into this in more depth in Chapter 13.

Back to the case of nurse Irene and little Tom. Why had Irene not performed a double check as was mandatory at the time for the administration of medication? The investigation committee found multiple explanations: she did not consider heparin to be a medication for Tom as it was only used to prevent clotting within the catheter; there should have been no other forms of medication in the room so nothing to confuse heparin with; it was a routine procedure done twice a day; and the nurse that would have to do the double check would have had to go through a full hygiene protocol lasting longer than the double check itself. It was a trade-off between safety and efficiency that I can relate to. Most other nurses would have acted likewise in the same situation. Mandating a double check in this situation as a safety measure to prevent recurrence would have cost a lot of resources. Such a measure, if implemented at all, is seldom found to be sustainable. As time goes by, the sense of urgency erodes, the daily burden is increasingly seen as ineffective and inevitably nurses start skipping the procedure until one day nobody does it anymore. The head of the ward wisely chose to reject the safety recommendation focused on double check, as recommended by the committee that investigated the incident. Instead, she looked for a more sustainable measure and found it in the form of replacing the ampoules of heparin by prefilled syringes with hep-lock. Now heparin ampoules can never be confused with other ampoules, as there are no heparin ampoules anymore. A good example of a physical improvement measure acting as a forcing function towards the required outcome.

So how can you prevent a reading error? Well, as long as reading is required, you can't completely. It does, however, help to realise how easy it is for you to misread. Just think of the email text earlier in this chapter. Being aware of your own inherent fallibility can prompt you to find support. Performing a double check the correct way, like I described above, reduces the chances of error. You could even ask the patient: "I realise this may sound strange, but I see so many medications during my shift and I want to prevent myself from making a mistake by misreading. Would you be so kind as to read out loud what it says on this label?" Tom, if he had been able to read, would have happily helped nurse Irene out.

HOW CAN THIS HELP ME TODAY?

Keep in mind that all humans can misread texts. Make sure that recognising crucial information, such as drug type or dose, is not solely dependent on your vigilance.

HOW CAN I INVOLVE MY PATIENTS?

Ask the patient to read crucial information, such as drug type or dose, aloud with you.

CHAPTER 3

Assumption is the mother of all screw-ups

THE CASE

For my parents' generation, a narrowing of the coronary arteries inevitably led to death. Medical technology has come a long way since. Placing a stent in an occluded coronary artery to remove the plaque and support the walls of the vessel, enabling the blood to flow properly again, has become a relatively straightforward intervention with a low rate of complications. Nevertheless, mistakes can still be made with disastrous consequences.

Enok Hansen was a 65-year-old, slightly worrisome but sturdy man with a mission. Whatever treatment he underwent had to be effective and efficient because he had to get home quickly to take care of his wife. They had been married for almost 45 years and still lived in their first house in a small village in the woods. Unfortunately, his wife had begun showing the first signs of dementia. Mr Hansen had a mission in life: he needed to look after his wife. He did not have time to stay in a hospital for long. I met Mr Hansen for the first time when the vascular surgeon consulted me. It was the first warm day of March. I distinctly remember because I had found time to eat my lunch outside in the sun. The surgeon paged me because the patient had developed chest pain in the wake of vascular surgery on his leg. I ordered an ECG that didn't show any abnormalities. I had his heart enzymes tested, and these were also normal. I explained to Mr Hansen that there were no indications of heart failure at this moment and he consented to wait and see how the symptoms developed. He was admitted to the surgery ward for postoperative surveillance. The following day his ECG and heart enzymes were abnormal and typical for a minor heart attack, of the non-ST segment elevation myocardial infarction (NSTEMI) type. I prescribed him therapeutic anticoagulants. In the following 2 days Mr Hansen sometimes complained he had chest pain. The pain could be managed with nitroglycerine. But after 3 days I had a bad feeling and, having discussed the case with my colleague cardiologists, decided that we needed more diagnostics. I called the nearest academic hospital to plan a diagnostic angiogram. This would show any blockages of the cardiac

13

arterial system. The following morning I was paged again, because the chest pain was not manageable anymore. We decided to admit Mr Hansen to the ICU, and administer nitroglycerine and pain medication intravenously. I called my academic colleague and explained that the situation had become more urgent. We needed to transfer the patient today. He agreed. We discussed the preparation needed for the procedure and decided to deviate from the normal procedure: we would not give the patient the antiplatelet drug, clopidogrel, yet, because he was still recovering from vascular surgery. Clopidogrel would increase the chance his wounds would start bleeding. They would administer the clopidogrel at the academic hospital, just before the procedure. With everything agreed upon, we had Mr Hansen transported to the academic hospital at the end of the morning. He was returned to our hospital the same evening and admitted to the ICU, as protocol dictated in these situations.

The intensive care nurse who had performed the handover with the ambulance personnel called me at home to let me know Mr Hansen had arrived. Stents had been placed in two of his carotid arteries. The procedure had been uneventful. Prior to the procedure they had administered clopidogrel so he did not need clopidogrel anymore today. When new patients are admitted outside of office hours, it is common for the cardiologist on call to come to the hospital and see the patient. Because I already knew Mr Hansen and there was nothing out of the ordinary, I decided to stay at home that evening.

I attended a symposium the following day and my colleague checked on my patients for me. The next day, Friday, I visited Mr Hansen on the ICU. He told me he felt fine and wanted to go home as soon as possible. He felt bad because his children had been taking care of their mother for so many days already. His surgeon did not feel comfortable with the surgical wounds yet, and wanted him to stay at least one more night. If the wounds were stable and his lab results were okay, he could go home on Saturday afternoon. Mr Hansen was transferred from the ICU to the cardiology ward in preparation for his return home.

My family and I went to visit my parents that Saturday morning to enjoy a weekend together. After dinner on Saturday night my colleague cardiologist called me on my cell phone. Mr Hansen had been readmitted to the academic hospital for an emergency procedure and had died on the table. I could not believe what I heard. My colleague told me Mr Hansen had fallen in the bathroom that morning. The nurses had helped him get back in bed and had measured his blood pressure. The blood pressure was so low, they paged the house officer. She ordered an ECG that showed a massive heart attack. They immediately alerted the Rapid Response Team and, after consulting with my colleague cardiologist who was on call, Mr Hansen was sent by emergency transport to the academic hospital. There they discovered that both stents were occluded by blood clots. The emergency procedure was too late and resuscitation was to no avail. Mr Hansen died from a heart attack resulting from the occlusion of both stents in his carotid arteries. When my colleague had finished, we both fell silent. I had not seen this coming at all.

"He seemed to be doing so well on Friday," I said.

"Yes," he slowly said, "but the worst is yet to come. We found out that Mr Hansen had not been administered clopidrogel after he was readmitted to our hospital. Nobody understands how this could have happened. It looks like this caused the stent thrombosis."

It felt like the ground had been ripped from under my feet. I promised to come to the hospital on Sunday to answer any questions the family might have and turned off my phone. For a moment it seemed the earth had stopped revolving. I could not believe what I had heard, it was simply not possible for us to forget the antiplatelet drug clopidogrel. We always administered this to our patients who received coronary stents. Always. Something must have gone wrong. My colleague must have forgotten to prescribe it, or the nurses forgot to administer it. Had the pharmacy made a mistake? How could they be so stupid! I felt anger swelling up. But my anger redirected itself from my colleagues to myself. How could I have been so stupid? It was my patient, I was responsible. My anger turned to fear. How will the family react? What will my colleagues say? I might be sued. Maybe I will have to stop working. Do I even want to continue working as cardiologist, am I fit for practice if I make these kind of unacceptable mistakes? Thoughts raced through my mind. Although I knew many of these thoughts were gibberish, I had lost control over them. I cannot remember ever having felt so bad, so lonely, as at that moment in the hallway of my parent's house with my cell phone in my hand and the cheerful chatter of my family in the background. I felt like crying.

REFLECTION

"Assumption is the mother of all screw-ups." I often use this quote from the action movie 'Under Siege 2' to help students remember this important safety lesson. In the case of Enok Hansen many things went wrong, but what I want to highlight are the numerous moments where somebody assumed that somebody else had taken care, or would take care, of an important step in the care process. Not all these moments had been visible for the cardiologists concerned. When the patient had been handed over by the ambulance personnel to the ICU nurse, the ICU nurse knew that the patient would have to receive clopidogrel the next day. She knew but did not act on that knowledge because she assumed her colleague of the day shift would organise this with the cardiologist. The cardiologist who did rounds on Thursday morning was also aware that clopidogrel was essential for the patient, but assumed that his colleague had taken care of this the previous evening, when the patient had been admitted to the ICU. After all, protocol dictated that the cardiologist on call visits all newly admitted patients and all cardiologists would have prescribed clopidogrel to this type of patient first thing. It did not occur to him to check because this was so straightforward. He did not notice that the antiplatelet medication clopidogrel had not been prescribed yet. The patient was transferred from the ICU to the cardiology ward where all staff have ample experience with this type of patient. So much so, that the ward nurse decided not to print the relevant protocol for the patient chart because this was such standard care.

Because of this, she did not systematically check all the steps necessary for this patient. She assumed it would all go according to protocol because they did this all the time. The cardiologist who did the rounds on Saturday morning was still under the assumption that the patient was receiving his required antiplatelet medication and, again, did not check. All healthcare personnel involved were distinctly aware of the importance of antiplatelet medication for this patient, but nobody realised that Enok Hansen was not receiving it. Meanwhile the blood in his stents was starting to clot and impede the flow of blood through his coronary arteries. His heart received less and less oxygen until, 2 days after his procedure, the flow was cut off and a vital part of Enok Hansen's heart muscle died.

We see a lot similar incidents in healthcare. Nobody double checked a patient's blood type because everybody assumed somebody else would, and then the patient unexpectedly starts bleeding profusely and the team doesn't know what type of blood to give. The correct hip prosthesis is missing because nobody checked because these prostheses are never missing. A well-known example in England is the tragic case of Wayne Jowett. In December 2000 two doctors administered the chemotherapeutic drug vincristine into the spine, intrathecally, instead of into a vein. Eighteen-year-old Wayne died as a result. Both doctors were filling in for the doctor who was treating Wayne. Both had limited experience with chemotherapy and both assumed the other had more experience. If one of the doctors had asked the other if he knew what he was doing, it would probably not have gone wrong. It is chilling to realise, in hindsight, how easily this fatal mistake could have been prevented. But at the same time, it is so easy to understand how the doctors involved at that time did not see it coming. We all make these kind of mistakes on a daily basis. I, for one, never check the head- and tail-lights of my car before I start driving, despite this being an explicit part of my driving licence test. Let alone ask my wife, when she is driving, if she checked the lights. Checking the lights every time seems undoable because then there are so many things I would have to check. Besides, they always work. And asking somebody else if he or she checked, feels like you don't trust them. "Honey, did you check the tail-lights before we started driving?" I doubt that question would contribute to a pleasant journey.

It just feels unpleasant to ask obvious questions, to ask something you think you know the answer to already. But if the answer to the obvious question is essential for safety, it's worthwhile to set your diffidence aside and ask anyway. Better safe than sorry. As psychologist James Reason pointed out, the path to adverse incidents is paved with false assumptions[1].

How do you evade this trap? First you need to be aware which steps of the healthcare process are critical. These are the steps, if forgotten or inadequately handled, that can lead to permanent harm or death of the patient. Clearing the cervical spine of a trauma patient is an example. The whole team, from ambulance to Emergency Room personnel, assumes the cervical spine is compromised until it has been assessed and cleared. Properly assessed, so not assumed that it's probably okay. They will never think 'the patient can move his head, so the neck will probably not be fractured'. Experienced healthcare professionals know exactly which steps of the healthcare process they work in are critical. This is what they have been trained for. Patients, on the other hand, often lack this knowledge. So in situations where the patient could be the first to recognise that a critical step is overlooked, it could be worthwhile to educate the patient on recognising this and pointing it out.

Next is to verify actively that these steps have been taken care of adequately. Or, as the Russian proverb that former USA president, Reagan liked to quote, goes: "Doveryai, no proveryai"; trust, but verify. During a medical procedure this can be done by stating the critical steps out loud. This is the fundamental step of the surgical time-out procedure. To state out loud that all the crucial parts of the process the team is about to embark on are in order. Do we have the correct patient on the table, have we prepped the correct side and site, is all the equipment we will need present? The surgical time-out, by the way, is an excellent example of how tenacious our default mind-set is to want to assume everything is in order. Many surgeons who have worked for decades without a time-out procedure find it hard to believe in its added value, despite the scientific evidence. It costs time, which they feel could better be spent on patient care. And in the past they never did a time-out and operations 'never went wrong'. The default mind-set in most humans is that they want to believe things won't go wrong. This assumption is continuously strengthened by our experience that, indeed, most things do not go wrong. The tail-light always works. For critical parts of healthcare processes, this fundamental assumption must be counteracted actively and persistently. You must assume that the process is compromised until you have enough information to conclude that it's not. The simple question 'can you show me that the clopidogrel has been administered?' would have probably saved Enok Hansen's life.

Luke Leenen, professor of traumatology at the University Medical Centre Utrecht, in the Netherlands, where I received the bulk of my medical training, understood this very well. He developed a way for other healthcare employees, be they fellow doctors, nurses or students, to speak up to him without diffidence if they felt he had missed something in his assessment of a trauma patient. He turned it into a game. He knew trauma patients were always complex and the chance of missing symptoms, fractures or other vital information is significant, however structured your assessment of the patient. So when the patient was stable enough to hand over to the ICU or a ward, he made it part of the handover to challenge the receiving end to find something he had overlooked. When somebody did find something, be it vital or insignificant, he or she felt no threshold to page the professor personally and tell him what he had missed. Professor Leenen had flipped the default mind-set: he nurtured the assumption that his team would miss something vital one day, instead of assuming the excellence of his team would prevent this. And he managed to mobilise the whole hospital to help him out. Pointing out flaws no longer led to shame or ego-battles, but became a feel-good opportunity to contribute to the common cause: ensuring the best possible care for the patient.

HOW CAN THIS HELP ME TODAY?

Assume critical steps of the healthcare process have *not* been taken until proven otherwise. Use the people around you, by challenging them to find what you missed.

HOW CAN I INVOLVE MY PATIENTS?

Explain to the patient which steps of his/her healthcare process are critical and how the patient can help check these steps are taken adequately.

CHAPTER 4
Be prepared

THE CASE

It's white and it stands in your way. The medical student. Doctors' humour, I had better get used to it because I was becoming one of them. But for now I was just a stand-in-the-way. My training in obstetrics and gynaecology, or OBGYN as they called themselves, was a breath of fresh air. It might have been the field, it might have been the gynaecologists, but finally I felt I was actually contributing to healthcare and I loved it. At first I thought it was a pain that I was allotted a hospital so far away from where I lived. To get to the train every morning before dawn was hell. But after a week or two, when I started to find my place, it became worth it. The nurses were nice to me, the doctors actually let me do stuff instead of just having me sit behind them on a round stool listening and they seemed genuinely interested in me. They even called me by name, instead of "Hey, you." OBGYN was also much more interesting that I had thought. It had everything, from birth to old age issues. Every life phase a woman goes through has its own obstetric or gynaecological aspects. Including death, as I experienced in the third month of my training.

Her name was Mia Kelly. I first saw her in the outpatient clinic, where I was tagging along with Dr Thompson. She was 55 years old and had been referred by her GP because of a gastrointestinal condition that had not reacted to therapy. For 2 weeks this condition had been complicated by urinary complaints. Dr Thompson took her medical history and performed a physical examination.

"Do you mind if I let my young colleague, who is training to become a doctor, also feel your abdomen?" Dr Thompson asked her.

"Please, young lady, go ahead," she answered. I examined her abdomen and felt a lump that did not belong there.

"We are going to take a look with the ultrasound, Mrs Kelly." Dr Thompson turned on the machine and prepared the probe for a transvaginal ultrasound.

"Look," Dr Thompson said to me when he had positioned the probe, "can you see it?" Mrs Kelly was also looking at the screen and I wondered if she could

19

interpret the black and white image enough to see what we saw. Even with my very modest experience in interpreting ultrasounds, I could distinguish a large tumour in her pelvic region.

After thoroughly examining the images, Doctor Thompson removed the probe.

"I'm also going to look through your abdomen, Mrs Kelly. I will need to apply some gel to your stomach and that could feel a little cold." Now we could see the tumour even better.

"I'm afraid I have bad news, Mrs Kelly. I can see a lump in your abdomen. If you look at the screen I can show you. Here you see it, from here to here. We will need to do more diagnostics to find out what this lump is. Please take your time to get dressed, then we will discuss the options."

Dr Thompson explained to Mrs Kelly that the chances were she had an ovarian tumour, but diagnostics would have to confirm this. He explained what the next steps would be. He would arrange to have her blood tested, a CT scan and a chest X-ray performed and plan an exploratory laparotomy for surgical staging. He clarified that this was a surgical procedure meant to determine if the tumour had spread. This operation was needed to determine the best type of therapy and was part of the therapy too. He would remove as much tumour tissue as possible during this procedure. Mrs Kelly was less shocked than I had expected. She admitted that she was already afraid it would be cancer when her GP had referred her. It was unnerving for her to have her fears confirmed, but on the other hand it felt like a relief to know the cause of her condition.

It was 1 week later when I saw Mrs Kelly again, on the gynaecology ward this time. She had been admitted for the laparotomy. I was there when Dr Thompson reviewed the CT scan. He had already seen the images some days before. He pointed out where the tumour bordered on the venous plexus, a large cluster of blood vessels.

"It's not so bad," he said, he could handle the operation. I walked with him to Mrs Kelly and he explained to her how he would perform the surgical procedure.

The following day I went to the operating theatre to see the operation. I donned my scrubs and when I entered the operating room Mrs Kelly was already on the table with the anaesthetist at the head. The team went through the presurgical time-out procedure and Mrs Kelly was anesthetised. Doctor Thompson made the incision. The gynaecologist-in-training was secondary surgeon. I was allowed to spread the wound. Suddenly, the wound filled up with blood.

"Suction," the gynaecologist-in-training ordered the scrub nurse, Astrid. I noticed how the little container attached to the suction device filled with blood quickly.

"Parveen, we have a bleeder and need more blood," Dr Thompson said to the anaesthetist. On the monitor I saw the blood pressure had dropped to 95/55. Heart rate was 110.

"All right, I'm giving her 2 packed cells and starting 500 Ringer's lactate," the anaesthetist replied.

"I think I know where the blood is coming from, I'll try to suture it."

Suddenly the blood pressure dropped again, now to 45/20. The patient's heart rate rose to 160. This was not going well.

"Dammit, people, what is going on?" the anaesthetist called out. "Astrid, give 3 packed cells and 500 ml of voluven. I'll try to get another 16 gauge needle into her." He stepped to our side of the table to place an IV needle in the patient's right arm.

"I'm not able to control the bleeding. We have to apply pressure. Get me a handful of large sterile pads. Student, come here and push hard. No, here, right here. Now push harder. That's good. Astrid, page the vascular surgeon and tell him to get over here asap. Do we have a haemoglobin level?" Dr Thompson was desperately trying to regain control over the situation.

"Hb 2.5, saturation 95%, we need more blood," the anaesthetist responded. "I hadn't foreseen this. She has a difficult blood type, I hope to God we've got enough for her." He pulled the phone from the wall and called the lab.

I was pushing down on the pads stuffed in the open wound, trying to stop the bleeding, while we waited for the vascular surgeon to arrive. When she rushed into the operating room 5 minutes later, the lab had still not supplied the extra blood. Dr Thompson explained the situation to the vascular surgeon. He suspected he had lacerated the pelvic venous plexus while debulking the tumour. I stepped back so they could examine the wound and continue the procedure. I could not see what they were doing, but I understood that they were going to leave a large wad of sterile pads in the abdomen, close the wound and transfer the patient to the ICU to stabilise her and fix the coagulation issues.

While we were washing our hands after the patient had left, I heard the anaesthetist complain to Dr Thompson that he would have appreciated a heads-up prior to the procedure on the complexity of the patient he had been assigned to.

A little later I went to the ICU to see how Mrs Kelly was doing. Her condition was still not stable. Her blood levels were very low, despite the multiple transfusions she had received. Around 4 o'clock she deteriorated. Her blood pressure dropped, her heart rate rose, her skin became clammy and she hardly reacted to my questions. With the ultrasound, Dr Thompson identified a large quantity of fluid in her abdomen. She was immediately transferred back to the operating theatre for emergency surgery. I heard the anaesthetist yell through the phone that somebody should get a move on with that extra blood. In the operating room I stayed back. The atmosphere was tense. Dr Thompson opened the abdomen and just seconds later I heard the continuous peep of a flat-line on the monitor, like I had till then only heard on television. They resuscitated the patient for half an hour, but without success. Mia Kelly had died.

REFLECTION

In my opinion, the main errors leading to the adverse outcome were that the gynaecologist had not sufficiently anticipated mass bleeding and that he had not communicated about this possibility with the rest of the theatre team prior to the procedure. A week before the laparotomy took place, Dr Thompson was aware of the fact that the tumour bordered on a venous plexus. It is well known among gynaecological surgeons that this location increases the likelihood of bleeding during a debulking procedure. Despite this, Dr Thompson did not structurally assess which measures he could take in anticipation of possible major blood loss during the surgical procedure. The anaesthetist was not aware prior to the procedure that his patient had a higher than normal chance of mass bleeding, which led to the theatre team being caught off guard when it happened. This was not a routine laparotomy anymore.

In Woody Allen's film 'Matchpoint', Chloe says: "I don't believe in luck, I believe in hard work". The same goes for medicine. Excellent outcomes are sometimes due to luck, but are mostly the result of hard work. Especially hard work prior to a procedure: assessing the situation, getting the team in line, specifying who is going to do what. In short, performing a thorough preparation to prevent, as best as possible, any unanticipated surprises that can negatively affect the desired outcome.

The French safety scientist René Amalberti once explained to me what the main difference is between pilots and doctors. Pilots are rigorously trained to follow guidelines and to avoid improvisation. Most of their required actions have been written down in guidelines and checklists. By minutely analysing all unexpected events, commercial aviation has been able to create a guideline for nearly every situation. If there was a fire in the cockpit, the pilot's first reflex would be to consult the guideline 'fire in the cockpit'. Doctors, on the other hand, are trained with fewer guidelines and are especially trained in their ability to improvise; 'every patient is different'. Working with guidelines is often scornfully referred to as 'cookbook medicine'. Change is coming, though, and we see an increasing number of doctors who appreciate the added value of guidelines. For these doctors, the guidelines are used as they are supposed to be: to get the standard stuff done as efficiently as possible and free mental capacity for the complex parts of a procedure[1]. In that vein we see a slow acceptance of so-called crew resource management (CRM), or similar types of teamwork training, in healthcare.

In August 2013, I was invited to visit the ICU of the Radboud University Medical Centre in the Netherlands. This unit had just won a national safety prize for introducing CRM in all the adult ICU units. They had been coached by Wings of Care, the company founded by Apache helicopter pilot and surgeon Marck Haerkens. I had heard Marck present many times before on the added value of CRM in healthcare. But I have to be honest, it was only when I saw CRM in practice that I finally understood what he had been trying to get across all those years. I witnessed the replacement of a central venous catheter (CVC); in itself nothing to write home about, but quite crucial to the patient. A consultant critical care doctor, a junior doctor, a nurse and a medical student stood around the patient. The cart was parked next to the patient and the junior doctor took a laminated form that noted all the necessary steps for the CVC replacement. As she went through each item, members of the team confirmed which part of the procedure they were going to execute and that the required materials were present. The team, and it really was a team, also discussed what could go wrong and who would take what action should this occur. Only when they had finished this pre-check, which took less than a minute or two, did they start the procedure. It went like clockwork, total control. I caught myself feeling a little envious of the student, wishing I had been trained like this. I'm certain I would have been able to make more sense of what was happening around me, if I had. That is in fact what CRM is all about: 'situational awareness'. Everybody who is present is aware of what is going on and what role they play. They know what's going to happen and what's expected of them. They operate like a team where each individual member is, and feels, responsible for achieving the desired outcome together. If one member deviates from the plan, albeit the highest in the hierarchy, all members are expected to point this out, even the lowest in hierarchy. The head of the ICU, Professor Hans van der Hoeven, confirmed this. "I would hold it against them if they didn't speak up," he said resolutely. The doctors and nurses I spoke to were all very enthusiastic. Not a word on 'cookbook medicine', but professional pride in their disciplined teamwork. And with unexpectedly spectacular outcomes. The prospective 3-year cohort study they later published showed a more than 50% drop in cardiac arrests and a three times higher cardiopulmonary resuscitation success rate[2]. Implementing CRM in the Radboud ICU had not been easy. It had used up a lot of resources. The whole team had to be trained, and the training had to be followed up regularly. Collaboration with other departments sometimes became problematic as those doctors did not want to conform to the 'CRM' way of communicating during handovers. Without the vision and continuous leadership of Hans van der Hoeven and without Marck Haerkens' expertise and unfaltering belief that CRM would prove itself, this experiment would probably have crashed and burned.

Let's get back to Mrs Kelly and the healthcare professionals who tried to treat her. Back to how the medical student had experienced Mrs Kelly's care process. Here one could not speak of disciplined teamwork, let alone of 'situational awareness'. The gynaecologist had found the ovarian tumour, had planned follow-up diagnostics and a laparotomy just like the guideline prescribed, but had neglected to run through the possible scenarios of massive bleeding during the surgical procedure. The theatre team had not been prepped on the possibility of massive bleeding, so when the patient started bleeding, the theatre team found itself 1-0 behind and scrambling to recover control. When the bleeding started, the gynaecologist was so focussed on controlling the blood loss that it did not occur to him that this might be the time to inform the team that the tumour bordered on a venous plexus and that this plexus had been lacerated accidentally. There was no checklist 'what to do when an ovarian tumour borders on a venous plexus', there was no local protocol on mass bleeding during surgical staging, so the doctors had to improvise. As a result, they were a step behind the whole way and, in hindsight, did not always make the optimal decisions. The committee that analysed this event concluded, amongst other things, that the anaesthetist should have administered fluids more rapidly. From the perspective of the anaesthetist, it is 'hindsight bias' to conclude that he should have acted differently. But not if you consider the knowledge the gynaecologist had beforehand. A week before the procedure, the gynaecologist had had information that would turn out to be crucial during the procedure, but had neglected to anticipate how important this information could be for the theatre team. Unknowingly, the gynaecologist had not enabled the team to take care of the patient in the best possible way. If the gynaecologist had been trained like Hans van der Hoeven trains his doctors, he would have prepped the theatre team on time to the possibility of massive bleeding. Then even the most junior team member would have been watching out for the first signs of blood loss. It is impossible to say whether the patient would have lived, but it is clear the team would not have been taken by surprise by an event which was, in all fairness, predictable.

Unfortunately we are not all blessed with a leader that invests in team training. There is, however, something you can do tomorrow to decrease the chance of becoming involved in a case like Mrs Kelly's. When I was a boy scout in Australia, I had a belt buckle that read 'be prepared'. It might sound corny but that is the key message of this case: Be prepared. Short and simple.

HOW CAN THIS HELP ME TODAY?

Discuss the most likely scenarios and communicate these with the people who can help you should such a scenario unfold.

HOW CAN I INVOLVE MY PATIENTS?

Discuss the most likely scenarios with the patient and make clear what he or she can do to help should such a scenario unfold.

In the case of Mia Kelly, involving the patient would probably not have been of much help. The possible complications of the procedure had been discussed and Mrs Kelly could not have contributed in stopping the blood loss. In many other situations, however, it can be of tremendous value to engage the patient.

CHAPTER 5
Speak up

THE CASE

After graduating from medical school I successfully applied for the training programme in otorhinolaryngology, commonly known as ear/nose/throat (ENT) medicine, at a prestigious academic centre. It was a small wonder I was accepted, because the competition was fierce. I believe there were over 20 applicants for the one position. I had worked hard to stand out. I had contributed to scientific research during my early training and was co-author of two publications on congenital deafness. My active 'student career' at medical school was also recognised by the selection board. I fit the profile. "I'll give you the chance to prove yourself", were the exact words of the department head when he called me to tell me I had been chosen. I was thrilled and a little proud, I must admit.

It was hard work from the word go. The work pressure was tough and there was no room to feel sorry for myself. A third year trainee who called in sick with symptoms of burn-out was publicly ridiculed by the department head in her absence. The smallest hint by one of the junior doctors that he or she was feeling pressured invariably led to one of the ENT seniors saying: "If you can't stand the heat, stay out of the kitchen." In other words: work, don't whine. I felt I could handle this. I recognised the culture from my medical school years. It's a game. Work hard, don't stand out too much and say something sensible at given times. I adapted and made sure I 'cut the mustard'.

After 6 months I went to the outpatient clinic. On every 4-hour shift 50 patients were booked in. Five minutes per patient. Because I was a first year trainee, I was allocated a maximum of 10 patients per hour. A full minute extra per patient, in kind consideration of my lack of experience. It was challenging but I loved it, it energised me. This was my life to come, this was the path I had chosen.

One day I saw a patient called Jason. He was 20 years old and had a history of chronic rhinosinusitis. He presented himself with a severe headache and high fever. He looked pretty sick to me but told me he didn't feel that bad. He had two roommates with flu who were both a lot sicker than he was, Jason said with a wry smile. He recalled he had had the same symptoms during previous episodes of sinusitis and was sure he would be okay after a couple of days of antibiotics. I wasn't certain. So much so, that I paged my supervisor, Dr Lopez. We never addressed the ENT doctors by their first name, that was not done. This was something I had to get used to, as most doctors I had encountered during my training had been fine with being addressed by their first name by their juniors. Dr Lopez was one of the older ENT doctors. I, like the other juniors, was hesitant to page him to ask for his advice. Somehow, he always managed to make you feel stupid. Even so, I called him that morning to ask him for his advice on how to treat Jason. I described the situation, the history and the outcome of the physical examination. I proposed to prescribe oral antibiotics and send him home with a follow-up appointment in 1 week. Dr Lopez was in the operating theatre. I imagined how the scrub nurse was holding the phone to his ear.

"And now you are paging me, because…?"

"Maybe you have a suggestion, I'm not sure…" I began.

"You're unsure? Want to elaborate on what you're unsure about, son?"

"Well…I…maybe I'm missing something here." I had a bad feeling about Jason, but something kept me from discussing my feelings with Dr Lopez. I'm probably over-cautious about this patient, I thought. Screw it, what was I thinking, paging Lopez about this case? What will he think of me now?

"Hmmm, you know what," Dr Lopez said, "why don't you handle your simple outpatient clinic patient and let me continue the complex surgical procedure you interrupted. Sounds like a plan?"

"Yes, of course, thank you."

Jason agreed with my suggested care plan and I showed him the door. I had a waiting room full of patients to see.

That was Tuesday. At the morning meeting on Thursday I heard Jason had died. His roommates had found him dead in his bed on Wednesday morning. His GP had informed the hospital in the afternoon. The cause of death was a brain abscess. The most probable theory was that his sinusitis had spread to his brain, causing an abscess, in the days prior to his death. I had missed it.

The next couple of months were the loneliest ones of my life. I was damaged goods. Dr Lopez claimed that I had not informed him adequately on Jason's condition. I had not made it clear enough to him that I felt something didn't fit the picture. Otherwise he would have come to see the patient himself, naturally. Rubbish of course, but what could I do about it? The other ENT doctors and the hospital staff were not in the least bit interested in my side of the story. I was on my own the day the parents came to hear our side of the story, the department head refused to help me out. "If you play with matches, you get burned." I should cross my fingers the parents don't haul me to court. My fellow ENT trainees gave me a wide berth, like I had some kind of contagious disease, as if my fallibility could rub off on them somehow. Everybody held their breath and waited for me to screw up a second time. At least, that is how it felt for me. I cancelled all my social activities and focussed totally on my work. I prepared everything twice and sat behind my computer all night looking up symptoms of conditions I might overlook in my outpatient clinic patients. After a couple of months the dust settled and everyone seemed to have forgotten my extraordinary status. I slowly started to relax a little and continued full steam ahead with my training. But I had, and still have, a scar that will never heal.

Later, at a medical school reunion, I learned the basics of transactional analysis. I'll probably botch it up if I try to explain, but let me try anyway. Imagine three circles on top of each other. The upper circle is the Parent-role, the middle circle the Adult-role, the lower circle the Child-role. Two three-circle columns face each other. These represent two people interacting. If one of them addressed the other from their Parent-role, chances are the other will automatically respond from their Child-role. "Clean up your room" – "No, I won't, see if I care". If one addresses the other from their Adult-role, then the other will most often also respond from their Adult-role. If one addresses the other from their Child-role, chances are the other will respond from their Parent-role. Responses strengthen each other and perpetuate that form of interaction. Through transactional analysis, adults can, for example, learn to understand relational problems they have with their father or mother. Once they see the pattern, they can try and break out of it by actively switching from the Child-role to their Adult-role. But one can also use transactional analysis to understand interpersonal relationships at work. My friend Ellsworth Cromwell was a few years older than me and had just finished his training in psychiatry. I'd made it to my second year of ENT training by then and had told him what had happened 6 months before. He listened to me and then took six beer mats, placing them in two rows of three. With a wet finger Ellsworth traced lines from one mat to another to explain the different forms of interpersonal interaction and how to get back to Adult–Adult interaction. How I could have voiced my concerns to Dr Lopez in an adult-to-adult manner. It was an eye-opener to me, but too late for my patient.

REFLECTION

Tenerife, Sunday March 27th, 1977, 1700 hours in the afternoon:

TENERIFE TOWER: Roger alpha one seven three six report when runway clear
PanAm Radio(c/p): OK, we'll report when we're clear.
TENERIFE TOWER: Thank you.
KLM FLT ENGR: Is hij er niet af dan? {Is he not clear then?}
KLM CAPTAIN: Wat zeg je? {What do you say?}
KLM FLT ENGR: Is hij er niet af, die Pan American? {Is he not clear that Pan American?}
KLM CAPTAIN: Jawel. {Oh yes!}
PanAm captain sees landing lights of KLM Boeing at approximately 700 m.
KLM CAPTAIN: [Scream]1706:50 collision[1].

All 248 passengers and crew of KLM flight 4805, and 335 passengers of PanAm flight 1736, were killed by the crash. It's nearly cliché to use this example when writing about patient safety because it has been used over and over again. But I choose to do so anyway, because this example and the lessons learned remain so illustrative.

The aviation disaster on Tenerife has been investigated extensively. One of the root causes was what they called the cockpit-gradient: the hierarchal inter-relationships within the cockpit that influenced the communication between the crew members. The KLM flight engineer suspected that the PanAm aeroplane was not clear of the runway yet. He voiced his concern, but this was disregarded by the captain. Acknowledging this as one of the root causes of the accident led to a worldwide programme of crew resource management (CRM) in commercial aviation. Nobody is infallible, not even the most experienced captain. Every member of the crew is potentially capable of recognising the signs of an impending accident before the captain does and must be empowered to speak up if they do so. Aviation experts also recognise, however, how extremely difficult it can be to speak up in certain situations and that it helps if the crew has a mutual understanding on how to speak up.

At the first patient safety conference I attended, in Halifax, Canada, one of the presentations was on the communication training at Qantas, the Australian airline company. To explain how it works, the presenter simulated an everyday situation. Imagine you are riding shotgun with a friend, let's call him Martin. Martin, in your opinion, is driving dangerously fast. There are four levels of communication you can apply, starting with level 1 and gradually working towards level 4 if the response you get remains inadequate:

Level 1: "Say, we are driving fast today…"
Level 2: "Don't you think we are driving fast?"
Level 3: "I think we are driving too fast."
Level 4: "Martin, you are driving too fast, I want you to slow down to the speed limit."

After the training, researchers examined the data of cockpit voice recorders to establish if the training had influenced the crew's communication. They found that crew members never had to go beyond level 2 to get an adequate response to their concerns. "Pretty steep approach today…" was often enough information for the captain to adjust his actions.

The message is: if you have a safety concern, you need to voice that concern for as long and as explicitly as it takes for the person whom you are addressing to react adequately to your concern. At the moment you have a concern, not when you are certain your concern is justified. Because often that is too late. In healthcare we are reluctant to voice safety concerns, especially in hierarchal situations. But also simply because we don't want to appear stupid. During his paediatric student placement, a friend of mine witnessed a surgical procedure on a pylorus. The upper muscle of the stomach of a small child was operated on. The view through the surgeon's microscope was projected on a television screen visible to the rest of the team. At a certain point the surgeon stopped and said: "Oh dear, that's dumb, I'm doing it the wrong way round." A junior doctor replied: "Yeah, I was already thinking: this doesn't look right." The scrub nurse also responded: "I was also thinking that you normally do it the other way around." My friend, being 'only' a student, kept quiet but realised he had also thought the procedure was not being performed correctly as he sat and watched the screen. So three highly educated professionals are watching a surgeon operating on a child in the wrong way and none of them says anything about it. This surgeon, by the way, was very approachable, the hierarchal relationship was no barrier for any of the three. They just all three thought the surgeon was the smartest in the room, and they were probably mistaken by thinking he was doing it wrong.

Another classic example is the senior physician or consultant who does not want to come to the hospital in the middle of the night. The junior calls him or her because they need help with assessing a patient or with performing a procedure. The senior deflects, averts or plainly responds that the junior has to do it him- or herself. If the senior still doesn't budge after using level 4 communication, you have this one last option:

"All right, I understand that you will not come to the hospital. I will now write in the patient's chart that I have consulted with you, that I have explained that this and this is the reason why I asked you to come and that you decided to stay at home."

Not a word of this is untrue. It may be scary to do, but it is always effective. Not many doctors persevere and stay at home if you do this. Just keep in mind, you are not doing it for yourself, you are doing it for the patient. Nobody can hold it against you that you are standing up for the patient. The other way round, if you do not voice your concerns clearly enough to have an effect, they can and probably will, hold it against you. The ENT doctor from the case story was not the first and will not be the last junior to be deserted by his seniors once a situation turns sour. He was left to face the mourning parents on his own. The ENT consultant had not come to see the patient, but the ENT junior took the fall for it.

Luckily, I have also seen positive examples. One situation during my own training still stands out. It was during my neurosurgery student placement when I was present during a cerebral bypass procedure. The patient had flown in from Spain to undergo the procedure because Dr Tulleken, professor of neurosurgery, was one of the only surgeons in the world who could perform a bypass around a brain aneurysm at that time. It was a whole circus in the operating theatre because many people wanted to see this. Professor Tulleken sat on a swivelling stool peering through a microscope as he operated on the patient's brain. I watched on the monitor. I noticed that he placed the graft vein, that would serve as a bypass, on the other side of the aneurysm than I had expected him to do. I voiced my surprise.

"If I may, Professor Tulleken, I had expected you to place the graft on the other side of the aneurysm first."

Professor Tulleken held his hands still, straightened his back and turned his head so he could look at me. Two calm eyes beneath brushy white eyebrows between a green surgical cap and a green surgical face-mask.

"You're right. I normally do. But I saw that this graft vein has small valves so I thought it would be better this time to place it on the other side first."

He turned back to the microscope to continue the procedure. Writing this down, 15 years later, still moves me. His composure, his control and the respectful manner in which he took his time, in the middle of the procedure, to answer my question on why he was deviating from the normal procedure; a question from the student, the least important person in a packed operating theatre. It made a lasting impression on me.

In the case of Jason, the ENT doctor wasn't sure what he wanted his supervisor to do. He felt a concern but could not voice this clearly. He had to have been pretty sure of himself to convince ENT consultant Lopez to come and see the patient at the outpatient clinic after finishing his surgical procedure. Sure of himself and not afraid of Dr Lopez. Unfortunately he was not sure and he was afraid. The relationship between the two was like a Parent–Child interaction: very dependent and far from equal. This interaction was nourished by everything the ENT doctors, especially the departmental head, did. If one person addresses another from his Parent-role, the other will most often reflexively respond from the Child-role. It is very common in healthcare that hierarchal situations impede communication about safety. As a healthcare inspector, I often see patient safety incidents that could have been avoided if the doctor had taken the nurse's concern seriously. It sometimes happens because the nurse is too timid, sometimes because the doctor is too aloof. In hindsight it is difficult to assess which of the two factors was most important, because, as we now know, the two reinforce each other. An aloof doctor will make most nurses timid, and timid nurses will make many doctors act aloof. The pitfall is on both sides. And both sides benefit if they break out of the Parent–Child interaction and interact on an Adult–Adult basis about their patient. In other words, interact as the professionals they both are. That is why I want to distil two lessons from this case: one lesson for the junior and one for his supervisor. You can take this a bit further: a lesson for the one who sends and a lesson for the one who receives.

The one who sends

If you have a safety concern, this has a reason. Remember: you are not crazy, you are not stupid. Yes, you can be wrong, but you are not stupid. So any safety concern you have is worth being seriously addressed. The wellbeing of the patient is much more important than whatever the person you are voicing your concern to thinks about you. It's professional, not personal. Forget how your safety concern might reflect on you, and focus on your professional duty to serve the patient's interests to the best of your abilities. In the end, this also serves the interest of the one you are voicing your concern to, because he or she is also invested in the patient's wellbeing. Speak up and use the four levels of communication Qantas pilots use. If needed, address the doctor by their first name to get their attention and to make clear that you are addressing them as one adult to another adult.

The one who receives

Work actively on creating an environment wherein all members of the care team, whatever their hierarchical position, feel free to express any patient safety concerns they might have directly to you. You just cannot oversee it all, you need the team around you to fill your inevitable voids. However great you are, you are going to miss something crucial one day. It's not enough just to expect your team to get through to you when they need to, it is your own responsibility to make sure you are accessible for them at all times. Openly invite your team members to voice their safety concerns to you. It's not cool to be aloof as supervisor, it's dangerous and potentially lethal. Besides, it's unbecoming, unprofessional and, if push comes to shove, blameworthy.

HOW CAN THIS HELP ME TODAY?

- If you have a patient safety concern, voice that concern as long and loud as it takes to resolve your concern.
- Actively mobilise your team to voice any patient safety concerns they may have directly to you, and always take them seriously when they do.

HOW CAN I INVOLVE MY PATIENTS?

Invite the patient to voice any concerns they may have about their wellbeing and always take these concerns seriously.

CHAPTER 6
What am I missing here?

THE CASE

This is a difficult story to tell you. Our son Tommy had to let go of life after just 18 months. Until 5 days before his untimely passing in the ICU, he had been healthy as can be. During his last days he was surrounded by us, his parents, but also by a legion of healthcare professionals: our GP, several junior doctors, a radiologist, paediatricians, surgeons, anaesthetists, critical care physicians, a neurologist and a pathologist. In the end our little boy succumbed to a serious salmonella infection that had spread into his brain. Medical literature, we have been told, suggests this clinical course rarely occurs and, if it does, the chances the patient will survive are extremely slim. Especially if the patient is an infant.

But still.

So many mistakes were made, that we can't help thinking Tommy could have survived if the caregivers had got their act together.

I'll walk you through it all, from the start, in big steps. On Tuesday September 20th we're not very worried about Tommy yet. He has diarrhoea and a mild fever, 39°C. It looks like a mild stomach flu. We give Tommy a paracetamol suppository. Looking back, we count this as Day 1.

The next morning his temperature has decreased to 37.6°C. Tommy eats a little bread with chocolate spread, drinks some milk and seems pretty happy, circumstances considered. But as the morning passes, he becomes increasingly listless and his temperature rises again.

In the afternoon Tommy has another episode of diarrhoea. At 3.30 I take him to our GP. He is worried and sends us to the A&E Department of our local hospital. There, the paediatrician who examines Tommy decides to admit him. He is administered oral rehydration supplements (ORS) to compensate for the diarrhoea. Tommy's temperature stays around normal for the rest of the day and night. But Tommy refuses to drink and his sleep is unusually restless. We are glad to see he drinks some lemonade on Thursday morning. We decide that I will stay at the hospital and my wife will take our dog to her parents' home. She is

33

taken aback when she returns and sees Tommy again around 4 o'clock. Our son is lethargic, complains of stomach pain, has rapid breathing and his pulse is racing. He does not react at all when a doctor inserts an IV line in his arm to administer antibiotics. His little hands and feet feel cold to us. There seems to be some fluid collection in his abdomen, an ultrasound shows. The paediatrician consults with an internal medicine specialist and they decide to consult a critical care specialist of a neighbouring teaching hospital. They conclude that additional diagnostics can best be performed in the teaching hospital after which Tommy can be admitted to the ICU there. Sometime after 9 o'clock that evening we arrive at the teaching hospital. But the diagnostics the paediatrician had referred Tommy for are not performed. Also, Tommy is not admitted to ICU. A student and a surgeon examine his stomach and conclude there is no need for any surgical intervention at that time. Tommy is sent from the A&E to the paediatric ward. On the ward he is administered fluids and antibiotics through an IV. That was it. They didn't even connect him to a monitor, even though the sensors for heart and oxygen monitoring that were stuck on him at the previous hospital were still in place. We don't understand what is going on and protest: wasn't our son referred to this hospital for emergency diagnostics and transferral to the ICU? Can nobody here see how sick our son is?

"Your son might seem very sick to you, but we have seen much worse," the junior paediatrician tries to comfort us. My wife demands to speak to the senior paediatrician. They tell us he will be around shortly. My older sister, who is with us and who has worked as a youth care nurse for many years, also demands that something must be done for Tommy. The junior doctor regards her as aggressive, asks her to calm down and does not respond to her plea. I find it difficult to admit now, but we were just too stunned, too drained also, to continue our protests. The paediatrician never showed up that night.

Friday morning, Day 4. We never leave Tommy's bedside because it is crystal clear to us that Tommy is getting sicker and sicker. By the end of the morning he is unresponsive and his temperature is 41°C. My wife loses it and in her helplessness she goes ballistic. "Why the f*** will nobody help our son, he's f***ing dying here! Goddammit!" She screams into the hallway.

That seems to have woken somebody up. Ten minutes or so later, suddenly doctors start pouring into the room: a paediatrician, a neurologist, then a surgeon, two critical care doctors and a handful of young'uns in white coats. Now they connect monitors to our son to measure his vital signs. The paediatrician takes blood samples and a nurse runs off with them. A radiologist does an ultrasound examination. The doctors conclude that Tommy has a salmonella infection that turns out to be resistant to the antibiotics they have given so far and has now led to two complications: fluid is leaking from his intestines into the abdominal space and the infection has almost certainly spread to his brain. They switch the antibiotics and add painkillers. After that, a neurologist takes a spinal tap and Tommy is rolled off for a MRI scan. Tommy is too inert to react to any of it.

Tommy is transferred to the Medium Care ward, and a little later to the ICU. Shortly after arriving at the ICU they connect him to a ventilator. We feel Tommy is finally getting the attention that he needs, but we also sense a lack of coherence. He is moved from one ward to the other, doctors seem to stumble over each other in getting the diagnostics they need. All these doctors of different specialties... OK, they seem to discuss enough, but it is unclear to us who is in the lead. We miss the bigger picture, the master plan behind all these different diagnostics and logistical movements. And what we find especially worrisome, is that the doctors focus too much on the short episodes when Tommy seems to recover a little. They see these small moments of recovery as legitimate arguments for a wait-and-see attitude. However, we feel they should pay more attention to the moments Tommy deteriorates because these frighten us enormously. What we also find very worrisome is that the doctors don't seem to have any information from the hospital Tommy was referred from. Whenever we ask what was in the referral letter, we get evasive responses.

After a series of peaks and troughs, we reach Day 5. Tommy is on ventilation in the ICU. It's around 11 o'clock in the morning, I had just returned from the bathroom and sat down beside my wife, when Tommy's heart rate and blood pressure suddenly decrease. Alarms sound and nurses rush into the room. We are gently pushed aside and, as if by magic, a whole team of caregivers appear around his bed. Tommy is resuscitated. The doctors try everything they can, but in vain. After 30 minutes the critical care doctors tell us that further resuscitation is pointless. The doctors step back to let us through. We each hold one of Tommy's hands as our little champion, the love of our life, passes away.

REFLECTION

There is so much to learn from this tragic case. However, I want to limit this chapter to two themes because these are relevant for all medical fields: reassuring family and handling referred patients.

Reassuring family – the fine line between supporting and belittling

"Your son might seem very sick to you, but we have seen much worse", was undoubtedly meant as support, but the distressed parents perceived it as belittling, as downplaying the dire situation their son was in. Certainly after it became apparent just how sick the boy was, this comforting phrase became a grievous misrepresentation. On face value, this statement by the junior paediatrician might not seem to be of any consequence for the chain of events that followed. But as I pondered on this, I became convinced that it was actually a very important moment. There are two sides to a statement like this: the effect it has on the person addressed and the effect it has on the person who says it.

It made the parents feel they were treated as overly worried parents and that the doctors did not take them seriously. This led to a feeling of helplessness and detachment from what was going on around them: they really could not believe things were happening the way they were. These feelings were reinforced by the doctors who did not respond to their repeated request for extra diagnostics. The father's sister was even labelled as aggressive when she joined her family's plea and insisted something must be done. It became an 'us versus them' situation. This created disruptive pressure in the relationship between the family and the caregivers. These particular parents were outspoken enough to voice their concerns and eventually escalate the situation. Many other parents or patients who find themselves in a similar situation are much less outspoken. They stop voicing their concerns, out of ignorance, modesty or fear that this might put a strain on their relationship with the caregivers they are so dependent upon at that moment. This creates a major patient safety risk. When two people disagree there are two factors that influence the way they handle the disagreement: their relationship and the subject of their disagreement. **Figure 6.1** depicts this schematically. If you value the relationship above the subject of the disagreement, you will be inclined to accept whatever happens to protect the relationship. I experienced first-hand how easily you can let the perceived relationship with the caregiver outweigh safety concerns. When my wife was in labour, I noticed that I could not see whether the caregivers adhered to the hand hygiene protocol properly. Sometimes I saw a nurse or doctor use the alcohol dispenser when they entered or left the room, but just as often I did not see them use it. I was a doctor myself, I had participated in many deliveries during my training, I was familiar with the risks of puerperal fever, I knew the story of Semmelweiss, I had been coordinating the patient safety programme of a major university hospital for years, I was finishing my thesis on patient safety and still…. I did not speak up. In retrospect my silence fascinated me. Why did I stay silent? At the time I thought "They're probably disinfecting their hands out of my sight," and "I don't want to disturb their work," and, if I am perfectly honest, also "I don't want to come across as a nagging know-it-all". I let my relationship with the team who was helping my

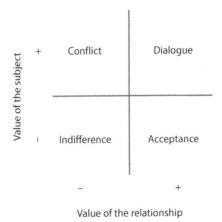

Figure 6.1 How disagreements are handled: subject versus relationship.

wife give birth prevail over my safety concerns. If even I didn't speak up, how can we expect less educated, less familiar, less verbally proficient patients to do so? This experience demonstrated to me how difficult it is for patients to voice their concerns. Especially in critical situations.

Back to the case of Tommy. "Your son might seem very sick to you, but we have seen much worse" is not an incentive to share any other concerns the parents might have. It is not an invitation for the parents to participate as active members of the care team. The doctor thus deprives the care team of a valuable asset in assessing the clinical situation of their patient. Nobody is better in distinguishing the little tell-tale signs needed to understand how a child is doing then the parents. This holds doubly true for mothers of infants. Although it is an understandable reaction for a doctor who sees (overly) concerned parents on daily basis, it is seldom the right reaction. Not until you are sufficiently sure the child is indeed not as sick as the parents think. And that was not the case with Tommy. Maybe Tommy's clinical deterioration would have been recognised earlier if the parents had been treated more as equals. The junior paediatrician could have said something like: "Your son might seem very sick to you, but we have seen much worse unfortunately. But that is also a potential pitfall for us. Please let us know if you at any time feel we are underestimating your son's situation." Take every concern the parents voice seriously, and either act on it or explain why you do not share that particular concern. This does not guarantee satisfied parents, but it does reduce the chance of overlooking something and it helps the parents feel heard.

The statement, "Your son might seem very sick to you, but we have seen much worse", also has an effect on the person who says it. If you say something often enough, you start believing it. Classic examples of this are adults who go through life with a distorted self-image because in their mind they keep repeating criticisms they received as a child. On the other side of the spectrum are the examples of successful companies that derailed because their CEOs had received so much praise over the years that they actually started believing in their own infallibility. The statement is an incantatory phrase to the sender him- or herself, "It's not that bad, I don't have to worry." By saying it, it starts becoming reality. I call it incantatory because it was not based on facts. Of course I cannot look inside the mind of the particular junior paediatrician, so I might be barking up the wrong tree. The reason why I stress this element of the case is because it relates to scholarly literature on High Reliability Organisations (HROs). HROs are organisations that have far fewer accidents than you would expect based on the complexity of their field, such as aircraft carriers and nuclear plants. A book I recommend on this subject is *Managing the Unexpected*[1]. The authors, Karl Weick and Kathleen Sutcliffe, found among other things that HROs foster a reluctance to simplify. If a problem seems straightforward, you are probably underestimating it. As long as you are not sure that a certain risk is contained, you must actively prevent thinking it is safe, because this thought is the first step towards the tunnel vision that will impede you seeing other relevant signals. What you say, and think, influences the way you assess the rest of the situation.

Handling referred patients

The second theme I want to highlight in this case is that Tommy had been referred. In the first hospital a paediatrician, a critical care specialist and a radiologist concluded that the care Tommy needed superseded what they could give him. They referred the patient to a teaching hospital for emergency diagnostics and intensive care. Having arrived in that teaching hospital, the patient was assessed by a student and a paediatric surgeon who concluded that the patient had no surgical indication. Only after having been admitted to the paediatric ward, did a (junior) paediatrician see the patient. The senior paediatrician who supervised this junior based his assessment on the information the junior gave him through the telephone and did not come to see the patient himself. They did not see the need for the emergency diagnostics the patient had been referred for and so did not perform these. The referral letter had been lost somewhere during the handover. In hindsight it is easy to conclude that both the junior and his senior grossly underestimated the situation Tommy was in. But it's more interesting to figure out what they could have done differently, with the knowledge they had at the time.

They had received a patient from another hospital, a hospital sufficiently equipped to diagnose and treat most sick infants. Nevertheless, the doctors there felt Tommy's condition was so alarming that they decided to refer the patient to a larger centre. The handover documents were lost. The doctors on the receiving end, in the teaching hospital, assessed that the clinical situation was not alarming at all. So much so, that the paediatrician did not even come to see the child himself. They hardly performed any extra diagnostics and placed Tommy on a regular paediatric ward for observation. The question these doctors should have asked themselves is: "What did our colleagues in the other hospital see, that we are not seeing now?" Asking this question would have prevented these doctors relying only on their own judgement. It would have led them to pursue the missing information. Never limit yourself to confirming your own judgement, always look for signs that contradict your mental picture. You must always keep in mind how easy it is for humans to overlook even the most blatant signals (remember the cardiologist in Chapter 3). This is not something to be ashamed of, it is something to be aware of and anticipate. If you find yourself in a situation like the doctors in Tommy's teaching hospital, where you just don't see why a colleague thought it necessary to escalate the level of care, then that should not reassure you but alarm you. "Why did my colleague judge this situation so differently, what am I missing here?" In Tommy's case that would have led to a phone call between the two hospitals that would have given the primary paediatrician the chance to explain his judgement call. I find it highly likely that this would have led to a different set of actions in the teaching hospital that night and in the following days. Nobody can answer the question whether that would have saved Tommy's life. Hopefully, you can save other patients' lives in similar situations by asking yourself: "What am I missing here?"

HOW CAN THIS HELP ME TODAY?

- Never reassure a patient until you are sufficiently sure this is justified.
- If a patient is transferred to you and you don't understand why the patient was transferred, keep looking until you find an adequate answer to the questions: "Why did the other doctor judge this situation so differently, what am I missing here?"

HOW CAN I INVOLVE MY PATIENTS?

- If you reassure a patient, ask if the patient feels reassured. Always explain in which situations the patient can come back to you ("If the lump increases in size, please come back directly.").
- Ask the patient why he/she thinks the other doctor had referred him/her to you and ask what expectations the patient has.

CHAPTER 7
Nine red flags

THE CASE

It was dreary and dark outside. The mercury had dropped like a stone since last night, so I pulled my beanie firmly over my ears before mounting my bike. It was my third night. After tonight, just one more and my nightshift would be over. Cycling through the deserted city, my mind wandered to the previous years. After completing the MRCP examination after my junior doctor training, I chose plastic surgery as my specialty. It cost me a year to admit to myself that the romantic ideal I had nurtured did not fit my experience in the field. Strenuous working conditions, desultory supervision by consultants who made no effort to hide their disinterest in teaching me the ropes and, how can I put this, strange colleagues. Maybe it was just tough luck. Maybe it would have been a totally different experience elsewhere, but after a year it became abysmally clear to me that this was not my path to pursue. I set up an interview with one of the professors of anaesthetics. During the few surgical procedures I was allowed to participate in when the ward was under control, anaesthetics impressed me. In my training till then, I had not done any rotations within anaesthetics, so I had never actually given this field of medicine any serious thought. Other medical specialists frequently made evocative, or downright degrading, comments on the perceived qualities of anaesthetics in general and anaesthetists in particular: they don't bear the burden of deciding which patients should be operated on, they're never the doctor in charge, they drink a lot of coffee and waste theatre oxygen, etc. And the jokes of course. One I must admit made me laugh was the one where an anaesthetist is flying to a conference when a flight attendant comes running down the aisle, shouting, "Is anyone on board an anaesthetist?!" The anaesthetist raises his hand and announces his presence, and asks what the problem is, and whether anyone is sick. "Oh, no, no one's sick, but there's a surgeon up in first class who needs his table adjusted." All this mockery had inadvertently influenced the image I had of anaesthetics. But in the operating theatre I experienced just how important anaesthetics is for the surgical outcome. How broad the speciality really is and how skilful an experienced anaesthetist becomes in understanding and influencing physiology. It fascinated me. The professor of anaesthetics saw my enthusiasm and offered me a research position leading to a PhD thesis, after which I would be admitted to the specialty training. I jumped at the opportunity. This conversation took place 7 years ago, and I had not regretted my choice for a second since. I love it. It's intellectually challenging, there is enough action and it provides a unique hospital-wide view on healthcare. The only issue is the nightshift. Yesterday, I was so dead tired it made me nauseous. I wondered if I would ever get used to it. I locked my bike and slipped into the hospital through the night entrance.

It was the fourth time I had been on nightshift on the ICU, so I had pretty much got the hang of it. During nightshift, there was one anaesthetist, in this case me, and one junior from another speciality. Each junior was responsible for three of the six ICU wards. Supervision was done by a consultant. On this night that consultant was critical care doctor Nicole Egan.

Nicole paged me around 3 a.m. to ask me to come 'line' a patient on ICU 5. ICU 5 fell under the responsibility of the other junior, but it was common practice during nightshift to ask the anaesthetist whenever a patient needed to have an IV line inserted, for the simple reason that the anaesthetist was the most experienced. I told the nurses of 'my' ICU I had to go and marched to ICU 5.

The patient on ICU 5 turned out to be a very sick patient indeed. A scrawny male with a haematological disorder, serious coagulation issues, respiratory failure and imminent circulatory collapse. The patient had to be intubated and before we could do this, we needed to put him 'under'. On top of this, the patient was seriously septic so we expected his circulation would collapse the moment we anaesthetised him. In anticipation of the drop in blood pressure, we decided to place a CVC so we would have an entry point for fluids and stimulants. We also wanted an intra-arterial catheter to measure the blood pressure accurately. Placing these two lines posed quite a challenge for us because the patient was deteriorating quickly and would bleed easily if we punctured him. As if this wasn't enough already, the patient could hardly lie still due to shortness of breath and anxiety. All in all it was obvious that the most experienced doctor should place the lines. That would be the anaesthetist; in this case that would be me. I am said to be quite modest by nature, but if I had to state one outstanding professional quality it would be my talent in inserting IV and intra-arterial lines. This had been told to me often by colleagues and it was a recurrent theme during assessments. So, although I was distinctly aware of the precarious situation we were in with this patient, I was not worried about succeeding. There was time pressure involved. The patient had just been administered FFP so this gave me a small window of opportunity in which his coagulation would be less problematic.

I started off with the intra-arterial catheter, which I wanted to insert in his right radial artery. My first attempt failed. I could sufficiently compress the haemorrhage this caused. My second attempt was successful. I was reassured about his coagulation because the bleeding I had caused in my first attempt had stopped reasonably quickly. So I felt comfortable enough to insert the CVC into his femoral vein. I can't remember whether using ultrasound to guide me had crossed my mind. I do know that it was not common to do so. I also know that I would certainly have used ultrasound if the bleeding I had caused with my first attempt had not stopped, because that would have meant that missing the vein would cause serious complications. A haemorrhage in the groin can get out of control all too easily.

Inserting an IV into the femoral vein is not that hard, because the anatomy in that region is very predictable. From the flank of the patient towards the sexual organ, you first find a nerve, then an artery and then a vein. At medical school I learned a nice acronym to remember the anatomy of the femoral triangle: NAVEL: Nerve, Artery, Vein, Empty space, Lymph canal. So what you do is search for the artery with your fingertips. The femoral artery is large and easy to find. When you've found it, you keep your left fingertips on the artery and insert the needle on the medial side of the pulsating artery. If you draw up dark blood that doesn't pulsate, you're in the right place. Easy peasy. Or so I thought. Three times I tried. Three times I clearly felt the artery pulsate, drew up blood that did not pulsate, but was not able to insert the guidewire into the vein. "Why can't I pull it off?" I asked myself. Each time I reinserted the needle only to have the same thing happen again. I was starting to sweat. At my fourth attempt I drew up pulsating blood. I knew I'd punctured the artery now. Not good. I stopped and applied compression to the groin. Nicole, who had been next to me all this time, took over and inserted the CVC in the patient's other femoral vein. She succeeded in her first attempt. Although I can't deny this hurt my feelings somewhat, I was primarily relieved we had secured an entry point for the patient.

In the meantime the patient was panting like a dog. I thought, "We need to tube him, stat!" The patient was fully lined up, so we could induce him. It happened just as we expected, the patient's circulation collapsed completely. We administered high doses of stimulants and vasopressin, progressively. The patient also had serious respiratory problems. I knew this fitted the picture of a fulminant sepsis in a severely immunocompromised patient. His blood lab had been measured every hour and we now saw his haemoglobin levels dropping. I immediately considered blood loss in the femoral region as the cause. We could not stop the bleeding on the ICU, we needed to transport the patient to radiology. So we hurried the patient, who had already been on his last legs and on top of that was now bleeding despite compression, to the CT angiography suite. That meant we had to push the patient through the hospital in his bed, dragging along a complete ICU installation. A patient who could barely breathe, a patient who you do not want to move around. It was an awful experience, and on top of it all I could not help thinking I was pushing around my own complication. It was 6 a.m. by now. I was on my way to the CT with a patient who was not my patient, who was suffering from a life-threatening complication as a result of my failed attempts to place a CVC. And I had to go along, because, being the anaesthetist, I was the one most capable of keeping the patient alive at this point.

At CT angiography we saw a blush in an aberrant artery. The radiologist concluded that the patient had an anomalous anatomy in the femoral triangle I had inserted the needle in. Where the vein was supposed to be, there was an artery that normally does not run there. That explained why I had not been able to place the line. We transported the patient back to ICU 5. There we called an interventional radiologist to set up the treatment procedure. My shift ended and my colleague took over. Dead tired I cycled back home.

I woke at the end of the afternoon and called my colleague to see how the patient was doing. He told me that the patient had been taken to the interventional radiologist in the morning with the plan to coil the bleeding artery. Once there, they could not find any active bleeding anymore. The haemoglobin level had also stabilised, so it seemed the haemorrhage had stopped on its own. Around midday, however, the patient deteriorated and succumbed to multiple organ failure due to therapy-resistant septic shock. I concluded with some relief that the patient had not died as a result of the haemorrhage I had caused, but I also realised the haemorrhage and subsequent transport to radiology had not done him any good.

REFLECTION

This case befell a friend of mine, I will call him Alex. Alex told me that it had drawn two types of reaction from his colleagues in the aftermath. The radiologist tried to sooth him. "These things happen. Insufficient coagulation is a symptom of the underlying disease. It was not your fault." The critical care consultants told him: "This is just how it goes sometimes, you know". Well meant, but in no way satisfactory for my friend. The second type of reaction was a technical one: Alex should have used imaging to guide him in placing the CVC because then he would not have missed. But it is not feasible always to use imaging when inserting a femoral CVC, so this reaction did not offer a viable means to prevent recurrence of similar situations. It annoyed Alex that he had to accept this could happen to him again.

At the time Alex told me about his case, I was working on creating a videogame on patient safety at the University Medical Centre Utrecht. The game was called 'Air Medic Sky One'. Players were trained to go on missions in a large helicopter that was basically a flying hospital. Part of the programme consisted of attending lectures in a virtual auditorium. These were short, 2–4 minutes, lectures on patient safety-related topics by various international patient safety experts. We had filmed these experts in front of a blue screen and pasted them into the game. One of these experts was Steve Harden and one of his lectures was about the 'Nine Red Flags'. Steve Harden is a former Top Gun instructor and CEO of LifeWings Partners, a company that helps healthcare organisations to translate safety lessons from aviation to their own setting. I do not have any experience with his company, but Steve is very captivating and convincing as presenter. I recommend you watch his brief lecture on the Nine Red Flags I uploaded to YouTube (search for 'AMS1 auditorium'). In this lecture he describes nine common warning signs that have been identified as key indicators of an impending adverse outcome in commercial aviation. These signs could have alerted the crew that an accident was about to happen. When four or more of these warning signs occur, the chances of an accident are significant. The nine red flags are:

1 Conflicting input: two sources of information disagree.
2 Preoccupation: fixating on one task to the exclusion of all others.
3 Not communicating: talking without this leading to the handover of the required information.
4 Confusion: when you think to yourself that what you have just heard or seen does not make any sense.
5 Violating policy or procedures: when you choose to violate a policy or procedure because you think this is best for the situation you are in at that time.
6 Failure to meet a target: a procedure goes beyond the scheduled time.
7 Not addressing a discrepancy: you see something that does not add up but you don't communicate this to the team.
8 Fatigue: normally you won't recognise symptoms of fatigue in yourself, but you can recognise them in your team members.
9 Stress: just as in fatigue, stress is something you can more easily recognise in others than in yourself.

An example from aviation is the crash of Turkish Airlines flight 1951 at Amsterdam Schiphol Airport in 2009, leaving nine dead and 117 injured. Two altimeters produced conflicting data (1), a command from the tower was incomplete (3), the co-pilot increased the thrust but the auto-throttle immediately returned the thrust lever to idle power because the first officer did not hold the throttle lever in position and it remained idle for 100 seconds (4), the crew violated the procedure that they should have commenced a go-around if the descent is not stable at 1000 feet (5) and the discrepancy of the two altimeters was not addressed (7). None of these items caused the crash on its own, but combined they resulted in the dramatic outcome.

Steve Harden tells us that the presence of one or more warning signs does not mean you will have an adverse outcome. It is just an indicator that the likelihood of an adverse outcome is increased. You should state the presence of a red flag as soon as you notice it and try to improve the situation or take measures to prevent the situation from escalating any further. "See it, say it, fix it."

When Alex told me his story, Steve Harden's lecture came to mind. Maybe this could help Alex. I sent my friend the video and this was an enormous eye-opener to him. He reconstructed that in his case there had been at least five red flags:

- Red flag 4, confusion: it was confusing that he could feel the femoral artery pulsate under his fingertips but could not enter the femoral vein.
- Red flag 6, failure to meet a target: normally he would have placed the CVC in one go, but this time he had still not succeeded after three tries.
- Red flag 7, not addressing a discrepancy: three times in a row he thought he was in the vein but could not insert the guide wire. Alex did not understand what was happening but did not address this out loud.

- Red flag 8, fatigue: Alex was tired due to the nightshift.
- Red flag 9, stress: he was under great pressure to place the line quickly because they expected the patient's coagulation to become problematic and because the patient's condition was deteriorating fast.

Alex realised in hindsight that there had been five signs that could have alerted him of an impending adverse outcome. If he had been aware of these signs, he would have stopped his attempts to place the CVC 'blindly' and reached for the ultrasound to help him guide the needle to the femoral vein. In that case he would have seen the vascular anomaly and switched to the patient's other side. Steve Harden's lesson gave Alex a way out of the two options his colleagues had handed him after the event: either just accept things can go wrong or always use imaging. He became aware that he was two points behind at the start of any nightshift: fatigue and stress. For that reason he would lower his threshold to escalate in similar situations, in this case to reach for the ultrasound.

I have never found a reference for Steve Harden's 'Nine Red Flag' theory. I would not venture to say there is a scientific basis to assume his theory applies for healthcare. It does, however, make sense to me. It helped my friend Alex make sense of the situation he had experienced and realise what viable actions he could take to decrease the chance of being caught in a similar situation again. For that reason I decided to include this chapter.

HOW CAN THIS HELP ME TODAY?

There are multiple signs that can warn you of an impending adverse outcome. If you recognise any of these, communicate this to your team and take measures to ensure the safety of your patient. See it, say it, fix it.

HOW CAN I INVOLVE MY PATIENTS?

Make it as easy and comfortable as possible for patients to speak up to you as soon as they might feel the safety of their care is compromised.

CHAPTER 8
HALT

THE CASE

Surgeon Patrick McCourt had had an exceptionally busy week. His theatre list was overbooked, his clinic overran on two consecutive days and the hospital had planned no fewer than three evening meetings, none of which was directly related to surgery. The longest meeting was on the electronic patient record that management wanted to implement. Patrick had been appointed spokesperson on behalf of the surgeons and this took up much more of his time, his spare-time to be exact, than he had anticipated. In training to become a surgeon, he never expected that as a surgeon he would spend so much of his time on non-surgical issues. All these things had kept him occupied that week, when on Friday evening he finally managed to be home on time for supper. His wife Kenzy had prepared a new dish, cauliflower and cumin fritters with lime yogurt, she had found in the vegetarian cookbook he had given her last Christmas. Niall and Todd, their 10- and 12-year-old sons, were already seated before the dinner was on the table, which seemed a first to him. Patrick skipped the glass of wine Kenzy offered him, because he was still on call. The patients on the ward had seemed reasonably stable, so he did not expect to be called, but you never know. As Patrick took a seat and smelled the dish, it hit him how hungry he was. Kenzy was serving out the plates when his mobile rang. Patrick sighed and stood up to find a piece of paper to take notes on. It was Doug calling, one of the A&E doctors.

A 50-year-old patient had been brought into the A&E Department by ambulance. She had fainted at home after she had pushed back her abdominal hernia. The patient had an extensive medical history. She had undergone gastric banding surgery for weight loss. A year later she had undergone abdominoplasty to remove loose skin and excess fat. Unfortunately this led to an abdominal hernia that they had decided not to repair for now. At certain intervals her hernia would protrude and she had learned how to push it back herself. She had done so this evening, but this time she had collapsed soon after.

47

Doug told Patrick that the patient seemed moderately sick. She could sit on the bed without support, but was uncomfortable and scored 8 on the pain scale. The hernia felt taut but was easily pushed back. The skin around the defect was red. The patient did not have guarding and Doug had heard peristalsis, be it slightly slower than normal. Percussion and palpation had been very painful in her lower abdomen. Doug had found no abnormalities in examining her lungs. Breathing was normal. The patient's blood pressure fluctuated between 95/50 and 130/75 with a heart rate around 110. Her blood showed a moderate leucocytosis and slightly elevated CRP and lactate. Arterial blood gas showed a slight acidosis. An abdominal X-ray and an erect chest X-ray showed no signs of bowl dilatation or free gas in the abdomen. The patient was not vomiting and did not complain of colicky pain, so Doug had dismissed ileus as the cause of the complaint but was not sure what else it could be.

Patrick listened to him. It was not an acute abdomen and the patient was not in a critical condition, so he did not have to come to the hospital, he concluded with relief. Most probably the patient had suffered a brief episode of bowel ischaemia after having pushed back her hernia. This would explain the pain and how sick she felt. They agreed that the patient would be admitted to the surgical ward for observation. If she remained stable, Patrick would visit her tomorrow morning. Patrick was glad it was Doug on the A&E tonight. How long had he been there already, 10 years, 15 years? He was already working A&E when Patrick joined the hospital. He was knowledgeable and reliable. And he didn't overload you with useless information like his colleague Ingrid would. Heavens, you could be on the phone for 10 minutes with her and still have no clue why she was calling. Patrick thanked Doug, hung up and returned to the dinner table. Finally something to eat.

That evening around 10 p.m. his phone rang again. Patrick had just dozed off. It was the surgical junior in charge of the ward. He was calling about the same patient. A nephew of the patient, a Dr Walker, had called the hospital and was very worried. He urged the surgical junior to do a CT scan. This nephew was a physician himself, a geriatrician working in the north of the country. When the surgical junior had explained to Dr Walker that he did not deem it necessary to order an emergency CT scan in the middle of the night because the patient was stable, Dr Walker pressed him to put him through to the senior surgeon himself. Could Patrick give him a call? Patrick agreed he would and asked how the patient was doing. Everything seemed stable. She had reacted well to morphine.

"You don't think I should come to the hospital to see her myself, do you?" Patrick asked.

"No, it's okay, I think I have it all under control here."

Patrick disconnected. He disabled phone number recognition on his mobile and called the nephew who picked up the phone immediately.

"I'm so glad you're calling. I don't mean to cause a fuss, but I'm just so worried. My Aunt Cora has a complex medical history, as I am sure you are aware. Troubled times behind her, one hospital admission after another. But the one thing she never does is complain about pain. So if she does, something is wrong. I don't feel comfortable about the way she has been treated since being admitted to your hospital. I would appreciate it if you ordered extra diagnostics, an ultrasound or preferably a CT or MRI scan. Your junior told me he did not deem this necessary, but between you and me, what does a young lad really know? Nice to talk to you. I feel a bit put out, picturing my Aunt Cora just lying there in a ward in her current condition without the doctors knowing exactly what's causing her pain. More diagnostics must be done, don't you agree?"

Patrick stayed silent for a moment. He had to process this flood of words and felt annoyance building up inside of him. Doctors are the worst patients, they always think they know better.

"My Aunt Cora probably has a strangulated hernia, I've seen that before with patients of mine. Trust me, we need a CT scan to make sure the bowels have not been compromised."

"I understand your concern, Dr Walker, but your aunt is really not as sick as you think she is. Her vitals are stable and she is reacting well to the morphine we gave her. A CT scan has no added value whatsoever at this point in time. The hernia was pushed back without difficulty so if the pain originates from the hernia, the peritoneum is a much more probable cause of the pain than the bowels. Yes, that can hurt, as you know, but it's no reason for any surgical intervention."

The nephew repeated his previous plea. The extra arguments he made did not convince Patrick to reconsider his conclusion. It rather made him a little cranky. What gibberish. Let Dr Walker concern himself about his own patients and let the surgeons of this world determine whether somebody has an acute abdomen or not. Why should he listen to this second-rate doctor at all?, he thought, but immediately brushed this thought aside, realising it was unjustified.

"Don't worry, we take our responsibility for your aunt's wellbeing very seriously. She will be okay." Within minutes after disconnecting the phone, Patrick had fallen into a deep sleep.

The next morning Patrick found out that the patient had been transferred to the ICU late that night. They had not thought it necessary to inform him because the critical care physician was present and had taken over the responsibility for the patient. An emergency CT had shown a perforation in the small bowels. A colleague surgeon who was on call in the morning had tried to operate on her but the patient died on the operating table.

REFLECTION

Looking back we can often conclude that a patient's family was right in predicting a patient's impending deterioration. In this case the patient had a complex medical history but, according to her nephew, never complained about pain. That she did so this time was exceptional and that made the situation alarming for him. The nephew had spoken up to the A&E doctor and had even been so bold as to pursue a dialogue with the senior surgeon, despite the late hour. He was a doctor himself, so maybe it was not as big a deal for him to call the surgeon as it would be for other family members, but still... He was very concerned but the doctors who treated his aunt did not value his concern. On the other hand, it happens much more often that the family is very concerned and the outcome for the patient turns out fine. The single factor of a concerned family does not always mean there will be an adverse outcome. It can be a warning signal, but just as often it can be noise or may even push doctors to actions that turn out to be detrimental to the patient. So the million dollar question is: how do you differentiate between signal and noise in the heat of the moment? The first step is always to take a concern seriously. Surgeon McCourt did no such thing. He tried to reassure the nephew, which clearly did not work. A detail that arose during the root cause analysis of the event was that the nephew was not aware that the surgeon was not at the hospital during the telephone conversation. Had he known this, he would have pushed harder. So how can it be that a highly trained, considerate doctor with no prior performance issues did not read the nephew's phone call as a signal to reassess the patient's situation?

A study published in 2004, in which almost 400 nurses were followed during 5300 shifts, showed that nurses who work 15.5 hours or longer have a threefold higher chance of making mistakes affecting patients[1]. The Joint Commission, a USA-based healthcare accreditation organisation, even issued a so called 'Sentinel Event Alert' in 2011, alerting healthcare organisations to the dangers of fatigue for patient safety[2]. In October 2010, when I was working at the Patient Safety Centre of the UMC Utrecht, we invited Chris Landrigan to contribute to our patient safety lecture series. Chris is a paediatrician affiliated with Harvard Medical School and Brigham and Women's Hospital in Boston, USA. He is a very enthusiastic and inspired doctor, who for a non-native speaker can sometimes be hard to follow because he talks so incredibly fast. Chris has done extensive research into the effects of sleep deprivation on the performance of doctors. Interns who regularly work 30-hour shifts turned out to make 36% more serious medical errors and five times as many serious diagnostic errors on an ICU than their colleagues who worked a maximum of 16 hours[3]. Also, completing a 24-hour shift doubled the chances of the doctor becoming involved in a traffic accident. In the USA, Chris Landrigan's work contributed to reducing the maximum amount of working hours for doctors in training. In many other countries, like my own, the number of hours a doctor in training works has luckily already been brought within normal limits. But medical specialists in private practice fall outside of this legislation and can work as many hours as they like. And a packed week, like the one Patrick McCourt was having, is rather the rule than the exception. Fatigue influences performance, in less extreme situations than a 30-hour shift. In commercial aviation this reality is acknowledged and pilots can indicate they are 'not fit to fly' if they are fatigued, for whatever reason. The Dutch College of Surgeons took a first step in this direction when they announced in 2014 that all surgical departments must mind the balance between workload and an individual surgeon's capacity and that they must all have a procedure in place for compensating strenuous on-call shifts[4]. To an outsider, this may seem a bit vague and unimpressive, but is a huge step from the macho culture prevalent less than 10 years ago, in which fatigue was simply denied.

A mnemonic I once learned is HALT[5]! If you are Hungry, Angry, Late or Tired: HALT; stop and realise that the chance you will make a mistake is increased. Use whatever means you have, coffee, a time-out, a consultation with a colleague, to decrease the effect of HALT. The main thing is to recognise the presence of HALT and acknowledge that this can negatively influence your decisions and performance. An example I discovered is that I make mistakes more often driving my car when I get annoyed by other road users. I had to miss my exit twice within 1 month before it hit me that it was my own annoyance that had distracted me from taking the exit on time. The same goes for hunger. Some say I get intolerable when I'm hungry. It cost me a couple of years and several unpleasant situations with my friends before I could admit this to myself. I have learned to recognise my own irritation or hunger and use them as warning signs that I have a bigger chance of making a mistake at that moment. When I was discussing HALT with Rob Bethune, a colorectal surgeon from England active in quality improvement for many years, he emphasised that the main difficulty with all of this is that HALT decreases your insight and knowledge of your own strengths. Simply put, you often don't know you're HALT and that's where the danger lies. You do, however, know when you are prone to HALT. Rob told me how when he was doing his surgical training and had young twin boys he would openly acknowledge during the preoperative brief that he had had a bad night's sleep and asked: "Can you people watch out for me?" He does the same thing now if he has been on-call the night before and is operating the next day. This is one way you can try to decrease the dangers of HALT for your patients.

An empty stomach during the conversation with Doug, the emergency physician, and irritation during the conversation with Dr Walker, the nephew, could have acted as warning signs for surgeon Patrick McCloud that he was vulnerable to making the wrong judgement call. If they had, Patrick could have taken a step back and reconsidered: "Am I certain that my mental image of this patient is correct? Have I thoroughly excluded the possibility that Doug is missing any important cues pointing towards an acute situation?" The first step would have been to go and see the patient himself and follow up on the concerns the family expressed. In another situation you could, for example, ask the nurse: "Do you have any concerns regarding the patient?"

Hunger, emotions, haste or fatigue can influence the decisions we make, and don't always lead us to the right choice. This is a human phenomenon. Just like darkness makes it impossible to see colours, hunger and fatigue make it difficult to think rationally. This is nothing to be ashamed of. However, it is something you can anticipate. If you recognise HALT in yourself or another, be open about it and realise that your chances of making a mistake are increased.

So it was not the conversation itself, but the condition surgeon McCloud was in during the conversation, that should have alerted him to read the nephew's concern as signal and not as noise.

HOW CAN THIS HELP ME TODAY?

- If you are Hungry, Angry, Late or Tired: HALT! Stop and realise that your chances of making a mistake are increased.
- If you see a colleague who is HALT, state your concern and ask how you can help.

HOW CAN I INVOLVE MY PATIENTS?

If you are Hungry, Angry, Late or Tired and this is influencing your interaction with a patient, be open about this and take a time-out. "I'm sorry, I feel I am not totally focussed because I am so hungry. Excuse me while I grab something to eat. I'll be back in a moment." Or, "I feel I am not at my best at the moment. Excuse me while I go and get a colleague to make sure we are giving you the care you need."

CHAPTER 9
Photo or film

THE CASE

I've always found 'take it like a man' a curious expression when applied to pain. Men can get so dramatic with the slightest twinge of pain. It nevertheless worried me to see Martin like that when I arrived home on Monday evening.

"I'm sorry, honey, but I haven't made dinner, I still just feel so terrible." It was almost a whisper, he spoke so quietly. The first half of the week it's Martin who makes dinner, the second half it's me. This agreement evolved naturally during the 3 years we had been living together. Last weekend Martin had fallen ill. Fever, headache, muscle ache in his neck and shoulders, flu-ish. He had decided to go to work today nonetheless, because he was in the midst of an important project that was on the verge of falling apart. Martin had been pretty stressed out about this over the past few weeks and personally I was not surprised this had now taken its toll on his health. It was my opinion that work-related stress caused his symptoms. Martin disagreed. He considered himself too rational to get physical complaints from intellectual work. He admitted to this being a stressful period, but it posed exactly the kind of challenges that made his job interesting. But that Monday he had not been able to continue working due to his complaints. He called in sick and hardly mustered enough energy to drive home safely. He was at the end of his tether. And now he just sat on the couch, with a bucket between his legs, blinds closed.

"My head hurts so much, it's unbearable. Tried paracetamol but threw it up. You go eat something, just leave me be."

At 10 p.m. I couldn't take it anymore. "Okay, Martin, this is no good for anyone, we are going to the GP. Come, I'll drive you there." We stepped into the car and drove to the out-of-hours service. After a brief wait we were seen by a female doctor who couldn't have been much older than me and who was clearly nearing the end of a long shift. She looked exhausted.

"Could it be meningitis?" Martin asked after the doctor had taken his history. He was lying on the examination table. The doctor pursed her lips.

53

"Is that what you are worried about?"

"I don't know. I feel so sick, I have never felt so sick before in my life."

The doctor examined his heart and lungs, took a pulse, measured his blood pressure and his temperature. She flexed Martin's neck so his chin touched his chest and then stretched his neck backwards.

"You have a fever, 39°C. Beyond that I can find no abnormalities. The results of my examination do not point towards a lung infection. I've also no reason to suspect a meningitis. I think it all adds up to a nasty case of the flu. I'll prescribe you some aspirin suppository. If it gets worse, please return. Best of luck to you."

The next morning I left for work early. Neither of us had slept well and Martin's condition had hardly improved since the night before. He stayed at home.

When I arrived back home that evening Martin told me he had visited his GP. Actually, his GP was not there so he had been seen by another GP. Martin didn't mind. He was never ill so he didn't really know his own GP anyway. The doctor had examined him but found nothing besides a fever. Martin had been prescribed painkillers and a medicine to suppress his nausea. It helped some, but his headache and neck ache continued to be hardly bearable. Martin felt like a wreck and looked the part. I called the out-of-hours to discuss the maximum dose of painkillers Martin could take and if they had anything to help him sleep. I could come around and pick up a box of diazepam. But it hardly helped. We had another restless night.

I decided to stay at home the next day because Martin couldn't even walk down the stairs anymore out of pure misery. We went to the GP in the morning. This time we saw his own GP. He also examined Martin thoroughly but could not find the cause of his complaints, besides a slight fever.

"It probably started with a virus and due to the pain you tensed your shoulders. Straining your muscles like that for 4 days, it turned into a tension headache that maintains and increases the pain. I suggest we try a stronger painkiller to break out of this vicious circle. If you agree, I will prescribe tramadol, which is an opioid, a kind of morphine."

The GP explained what the side-effects could be and in which instances we should contact him again. We drove to the pharmacy to pick up the medication and returned home where I helped Martin on the couch.

After lunch, which I ate alone, Martin's condition had remained unchanged. The pain had not decreased. This was the limit for me. I hauled Martin into the car and drove back to the GP. He was doing house calls so we were seen by yet another doctor. Once again we told the whole story and the doctor did her examinations. Blood pressure, heart rate, shone a light in Martin's eyes and moved Martin's head in all directions, which made him nauseous. Her conclusion was identical: virus and tension headache. She more or less gave the same instructions as Martin's GP had and added a muscle relaxant to the list of medications.

That night I could take it no longer. This was not normal anymore, I had never seen Martin this sick for so long. I dragged him to the car and drove to the out-of-hours. We were seen by a new doctor. This time I told the story from start to finish. The doctor examined Martin and, although he did not find anything new, he did not trust the situation. He referred Martin to the hospital, which was adjacent to the out-of-hours clinic. At the A&E Department the doctors concluded that Martin had meningitis. I was shocked. He was promptly admitted and given an intravenous drip. I collapsed into the chair next to his bed. Drained, worried and scared, but grateful that he finally received the care he needed. I fell asleep in the chair.

REFLECTION

When I told my former colleague Dorien Zwart about my ideas for this book, she immediately said: "For GPs in the out-of-hours service, one of the biggest pitfalls is that you only get to see a snapshot of the patient in front of you, not the whole picture. That makes it very easy to misinterpret the disease." Dorien is a GP and assistant professor. We collaborated for some years at the Patient Safety Centre where she was working on her PhD thesis on incident reporting in primary care. "I've seen so many incident reports describing situations in which you can clearly see the progression of the symptoms in hindsight. But this progression was missed because the patient was seen by different doctors each time. The doctors had no comparison so they each saw a stable snapshot and overlooked the patient's deterioration over time."

Inspired by the lectures her colleague GP Alfred Sachs gives on chronic illness in primary care, Dorien makes the comparison between a photo and a film. You judge symptoms and diagnostics in the context of the moment, as if the patient is in a photograph, while in fact this picture is just a 'still' from the film, the motion picture, about this patient. A patient's illness is not a photo, but a film. There are dynamics that are hidden from sight once the film is frozen into the frame of a doctor's visit. This goes for chronic diseases, and often also for missed diagnoses.

The same phenomenon takes place in everyday life outside of healthcare. When I was writing the original version of this book, my children were 2 and 4 years old. I am blessed with plenty of opportunity to see my kids during the day. I often think of those parents who only get to see their kids after work, who only see the snapshot between 7 and 8 p.m. I feel for these parents, because they must think they have terrible children. Always tired, quick to cry, disinterested in anything except television or the iPad. Not a pretty picture. While the film is much happier.

In Martin's case there were a total of six doctors who saw him in a period of 3 days. Five examined Martin, one only spoke with his girlfriend on the phone. Each doctor saw just a snapshot of the course of his illness. Some had access to his patient record and could see what the doctors before them had concluded and done. But because the symptoms were basically the same over time (fever, headache, neck ache) and the severity of these symptoms had not been objectified and written down, there was no way of seeing progression over time. GP number four, for example, did not notice that the headache had increased from a six to an eight on the pain scale, because it was not common practice for GPs to rate pain with a pain scale like they do in hospitals. She only saw a patient who had had a headache since the weekend that did not react sufficiently to the first choice painkillers.

If the same doctor had seen Martin three times, this doctor would probably have referred Martin to a hospital, if only because it would strike her as alarming that a young and otherwise healthy man was sitting in front of her for the third time in 3 days. Because this doctor would have had two points of reference, she would have had less trouble recognising the deterioration of the patient. She would have seen a form of progression that did not fit the diagnosis of tension headache.

One can already find examples in healthcare where purposeful efforts are made to turn a series of photos into a film. Psychiatrists use the Hamilton scale for depression. This scale is not meant for diagnosing depression, but for creating insight into the progression of the depression. The Hamilton is a tool for stepping out of the photo and into the film. Recording the answers a patient gives is somewhat subject to interpretation, which makes the Hamilton more reliable if the same psychiatrist fills it out each time. Another example is the growth charts used by paediatricians. These charts consist of a series of percentile curves that illustrate the distribution of length and weight in children. Using these charts, you can track whether a child is small or large for its age and, more importantly, if it is growing at the rate it is supposed to. The measurements over time create a curve of the child's growth, thereby creating a sort of film, making changes in the rate of growth visible.

Back to the case. How could one of the GPs have stepped out of the photo and into the film? Maybe just using this metaphor might have helped. That would have made the doctor look for changes in relation to the earlier visits to the doctors. If possible, the doctor might have tried to contact one of the previous doctors to confer. "I'm seeing this patient that you saw earlier. You interpreted his complaints as tension headache but the therapy you prescribed has had no effect. Did you consider other causes that might be more plausible now, considering this extra information?" Out of hours it is probably not feasible to get to speak to the other doctor. But just considering this option might already have helped prevent the GP from continuing blindly along the path that the previous doctor had put the patient on. You could say it's about creating 'situational awareness', which I touched on earlier, in Chapter 4. Being aware of the situation you are in and of the role you play. Realising you are part of a team, in this case the other members being the doctors who had seen the patient before you, and that each team member bears a responsibility for reaching the common goal. Studies of commercial aviation showed that 88% of the accidents involving human error could be attributed to problems with situational awareness[1]. It is becoming increasingly clear that healthcare is struggling with similar issues. Studies of safety in operating theatres showed that most intraoperative incidents were related to poor situational awareness[2]. Research by Hardeep Singh showed that lack of situational awareness also contributes to diagnostic errors in primary care[3]. He describes four levels of situational awareness (**Figure 9.1**):

- Level 1: Data perception (what is the information?).
- Level 2: Comprehension of relevant data (what does this information mean?).
- Level 3: Forecast future events (what is likely to occur?).
- Level 4: Awareness of the best path to follow (what exactly shall I do next?).

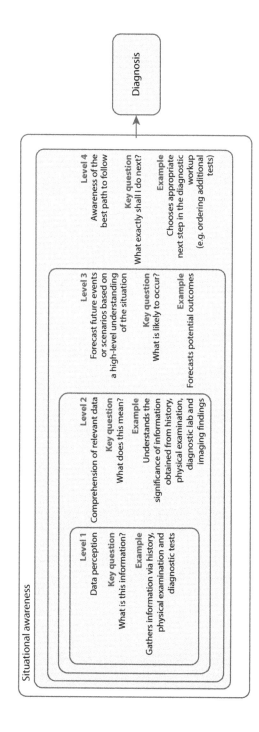

Figure 9.1 Adaptation of Endsley's model of situational awareness to medical diagnosis. Note: information from lower levels feeds forward into higher levels, and information from higher levels feeds back into lower levels. (From Singh H, Davis Giardina T, Petersen LA, et al. Exploring situational awareness in diagnostic errors in primary care. *BMJ Qual Saf* 2012;**21**(1):30–8.)

Using the photo–film analogy helps you run through these four levels conscientiously. It makes you take previous information into consideration, not just the information at hand. It helps place the current information in the stream of events and thus create a moving picture forecasting future events. This leads to level 4, an action plan. In Martin's case, the GPs asked his medical history, asked about his current complaints and performed a physical examination including basic diagnostics, such as temperature and blood pressure. Based on this information they deduced the most likely cause, which led to an action plan. So it would seem they covered all four levels Hardeep Singh describes. If one had benchmarked the GPs' actions against the four levels, without knowledge of the outcome, they would have appeared to have had adequate situational awareness. However, this did not turn out to be the case. What else could the GPs have done? I suspect there is another element of importance in assessing the four levels of situational awareness and in using the photo–film analogy: the protagonist, the main character of the 'film'.

I suspect the GPs ran through the four levels of situational awareness with themselves, subconsciously, as the protagonist. Not with the patient as protagonist. If the doctors had any notion of a film analogy at all, I bet the doctor was the main character and the patients were supporting actors at best, pictures passing by. And I could understand completely, because these doctors had all seen multiple patients that day. In such situations it is only human to use solution-orientated thinking, such as, "There is a patient in front of me, what am I going to do next?", instead of more abstract thinking, such as, "I am just a supporting actor in this patient's film, how can my role fit in with the previous scene?". Don Berwick, one of the founders of the USA-based Institute of Healthcare Improvement, once phrased it like this: "[We] would all be far better off if we professionals recalibrated our work such that we behaved with patients and families not as hosts in the care system, but as guests in their lives"[4]. A patient is not our guest, we are guests in the life of our patient. Berwick claims this should be the mantra of patient-centred care. I believe this mantra resonates with the main lesson from Martin's case. The doctor should exchange his or her subconscious idea that the patient is a supporting actor in the doctor's film, to awareness of the actual situation – that the doctor plays but a mere supporting role in the film of the patient's life.

To assess properly the medical situation of a patient you only briefly see, you need to consider this patient as the protagonist of their own film. The scene the second GP figured in was not 'Martin is sick', but 'sick Martin is being seen by yet another GP because the action plan of the previous GP had too little effect'. Then the GP would have acted differently from level 1 onwards. That doctor would have been more aware of the situation that there had been a plan of action (painkillers) that did not have the intended effect. Instead of continuing down the same path (more painkillers) he could have reassessed the situation. Put more simply, the GP would have realised at an earlier stage that the therapy was not working as expected and thus that they were possibly treating the wrong disease. With that realisation, the GP would have probably referred Martin to a hospital much sooner.

In healthcare we often see serious adverse events made possible by healthcare professionals being insufficiently aware of the situation they are in and the role they are playing. I believe healthcare professionals can improve their so-called 'situational awareness' if they view the illness of patient they are treating not as a photo, but as a film, with the patient as protagonist.

HOW CAN THIS HELP ME TODAY?

If you see a patient only once, realise that you are just seeing a photo while the course of the disease is a film.

HOW CAN I INVOLVE MY PATIENTS?

Describe to the patient what you are seeing and ask how this differs from his or her previous visit.

CHAPTER 10
Risk accumulation

THE CASE

Saturday November 6th 2015 was the worst day of my life. I'm writing this all down afterwards, hoping it will somehow help placate me. Most events that day will remain with me till the day I die. My husband, cursed with a photographic memory, helped fill out the blanks, the moments I was too far gone to be aware of what was happening around me. The only part neither of us witnessed was the emergency procedure in the operating theatre. I was anaesthetised and my husband, Awraham, was not allowed in. But we don't have any complaints about the surgical procedure, as opposed to the preceding events that were fraught with erroneous judgement calls. A veritable healthcare meltdown, as Awraham would later describe it.

It's Saturday, my fourth day in the hospital. I have been pregnant exactly 42 weeks now. During the previous days many things had already gone wrong from our point of view. The ordeal started when my cervix did not keep up with the rest of my body's plan to give birth. The gynaecologist, who only briefly showed up when the midwife expressly asked him to, kept talking about an 'unripe portio'. At home my blood pressure had been raised, but in the hospital this had dropped down to normal levels. Looking back, that might have been the only bright spot in my whole story.

On Tuesday, the day before I was admitted, they found out my water was decreasing more than it should. I have no idea what the significance of this observation is. But I suspect that a combination of a low amniotic volume in combination with my unripe cervix led to the atrocious pain I suffered when they applied vaginal gel to induce labour. This was done four times in total during my hospital stay. Three days in a row. Around the second time, on Wednesday, my waters broke. Every time they gave me the gel I protested and could not stop myself crying in pain. I hit rock bottom on Friday when they not only applied gel but also introduced a balloon. The idea was to fill the balloon with water and so help my cervix dilate. Unfortunately it was not possible to fill the balloon adequately

61

because the slightest volume made me cringe in pain. And I don't consider myself oversensitive; I broke my arm once and hardly cried.

Not long after being admitted, the midwife hooked me up to a CTG monitor to record the uterine contractions. The machine didn't measure a proper contraction once, for the simple reason that I had none. But the CTG was also meant to record the fetal heartbeat and this is exactly where it went miserably wrong on Saturday.

Until this day I don't know what to believe. The gynaecologist had twice promised me I would undergo a caesarean on Saturday if my cervix had not opened up enough by then. But the 'lesser gods' around me say a caesarean is usually planned before or after the weekend, due to staffing issues.

However it may be, on Saturday morning I feel weighed down by an overwhelming lassitude, having endured yet another night with hardly any sleep. And I am in tremendous pain. I asked the ward nurse to remove the balloon. This is not within her remit and she confers with the gynaecologist. She lets me know he felt it better to keep the balloon in place to reduce the chance a caesarean would be needed. Morphine is not an option to reduce my pain. "It won't help. It will cause your contractions to subside and will only make you drowsy." I seem to be the only person in the room who has lost faith in a natural delivery. Maybe because it's my first and I have the least experience of everybody around me? At 8 a.m. the nurse finally removes the balloon. Once again pain shoots through my body. But I am also relieved this farce had come to an end. The midwife checks my dilatation and, lo and behold, it has reached 3 cm. So the pain last night was not for nothing?

My brief bout of happiness is short lived, when the midwife and I both see the green smear in my sanitary pad. What is that? Nobody will tell me. And I don't have time to pursue my question because, finally, I am transferred from the ward to the delivery room. They attach me to a drip and reposition the CTG. It seems like forever that they discuss the pros and cons of an epidural. When they've finally made a positive decision, they don't follow through because they say it's too early for a caesarean.

Awrahan and I have trouble keeping quiet. It has taken so long already. On Tuesday the gynaecologist had told us it was time for the baby to be born. It has been 4 days since then, already. On Thursday my husband and I both had a bad feeling and expressed this to the gynaecologist. He promised we would try for another 24 hours max and if my cervix was not ready by then, would switch over to a surgical delivery. That was 36 hours ago. I'm now in my fourth day in the hospital and my cervix has still only opened a measly 3 cm. In our opinion all odds are stacked against a natural delivery. We now know that the green smear was what they call meconium, our baby's excrement. With the removal of the balloon, the last bit of water also left the womb. We are terribly concerned about the wellbeing of our baby. On the CTG monitor we regularly see his heartbeat drop and sometimes even disappear. The midwife runs into the room and says I should turn on my back, at the same time trying to reassure us by saying it was only a 'deceleration', a temporary drop in an otherwise normal heart rate.

Her reassurances do not reassure us at all, certainly not after the CTG peeps fall silent after I turn on my back as she told me to do. When I turn on my right side, against her specific instructions, our baby's heartbeat recovers. The first time after this happens, they attach a new medication to my drip. After the third time this happens, they stop the uterine stimulants and administer some other drug. Twenty minutes later they restart the uterine stimulants and shortly after we see another drop in our baby's heart rate. I'm starting to panic now. "For heaven's sake, please just stop all this and do the caesarean!" Earlier this week the gynaecologist would have none of it.

"Too dangerous, an unnecessary risk," he stated.

"How dangerous?" I persisted.

"You could die," he literally said. But at this moment I am not afraid of dying, all I want is my baby to live.

Evidently the stakes had to get higher before any action could be taken. On Saturday, at exactly 3 p.m., 7 hours after being rolled into the delivery room, our baby's heart stops again. And it stays still. We see no reaction from the room where the midwives should be monitoring the CTG. There's nobody there, my husband discovers. I push the alarm button, Awraham runs back into the hallway and calls out for help. Now suddenly everything happens at once. Nurses arrive, the midwife pages the gynaecologist. He rushes into the room in no time and in staccato voice briefs us that I will be taken to theatre for an emergency caesarean. And before I know it, I am anaesthetised.

I'm hardly awake when I hear what I desperately did not want to hear. Our son is not well. He had perinatal hypoxia, an oxygen deficiency during birth. It might have happened in the womb, it might have happened during the caesarean.

"Is he alive?"

"Yes, he's alive but he had to be resuscitated. He is upstairs in paediatric intensive care. His condition is serious, I'm afraid. Your husband is with him now."

That evening we discover that Bram's condition is not serious, but critical. He must have been covered in meconium in the womb. It had even entered his lungs. They had sucked it all out. Maybe that's why he didn't get enough oxygen. The paediatricians are doing everything they possibly can. They even cool Bram to prevent possible brain damage from getting worse. But all to no avail. In the early hours of Sunday our little boy, our precious little hero, dies in our arms.

During 42 weeks of my pregnancy I carried a healthy child. But now we have only a grave to show for it. The last 24 hours of my pregnancy were a nightmare, actually the whole last week was a horror film come true. Can anybody explain to us what went wrong?

REFLECTION

Bram's mother never received an answer to her question, despite the many experts who looked over her case. The healthcare professionals involved, including the obstetricians/gynaecologists, concluded that nothing had gone wrong in the medical technical domain. During a meeting some weeks after the event where they discussed the case, the obstetricians told the parents that they would make the same decisions again if confronted with similar circumstances. They were deeply moved by the unexpected outcome, but convinced they had done nothing wrong. Their conclusion was confirmed by the hospital committee that investigated the event: "The outcome could not have been prevented. (…) The healthcare professionals adhered to the relevant professional guidelines during the whole sequence of events." Above all, Bram's parents wanted the hospital to prevent other parents having to go through a similar ordeal. They wanted the hospital to learn from this event and take measures to ensure that the care process would be safer from now on. The conclusion that nothing could be improved astounded them and, they felt, was utterly unacceptable.

The hospital arranged for an external expert to go over the case, a very experienced and highly regarded obstetrician. This expert concluded that the cardiotocography (CTG) had shown no abnormalities until the day of the delivery and that there had been no signals indicating the child was in danger. There had been no reason to convert to a caesarean. The abnormal CTGs on the day of birth should have led to the doctors performing further diagnostics by fetal scalp blood sampling (FBS). Not being able to perform FBS could have been an indication for a caesarean. However, the expert could see why the obstetrician involved did not think an FBS necessary because the fetal heart rate recovered quickly as soon as the mother shifted position. In other words, the external expert also concluded that the adverse outcome had been unavoidable.

Sadly enough I have seen multiple cases very similar to this one, reported to the Dutch Healthcare Inspectorate. Subtle differences in the details, but the same pattern of calculated risks, a deceased or crippled child and content experts who conclude in hindsight that the professionals involved had adequately adhered to the relevant guidelines. I am no obstetrician, so I am treading on dangerous ground when I suggest there might be more to it. There might be something to learn from these cases after all, which could decrease the chance of similar dramatic outcomes. To me, the crux of the matter lies in the accumulation of risks. You should not weigh each risk separately, but weigh them together, in the context, and so create a full picture of how much risk the patient is in at that moment of time. A picture you keep updating as the risks evolve.

Shell, the oil company, developed the 'Rule of Three'. A 2-page leaflet explains how this technique can help employees realise how normal situations can escalate to become serious risks and how this can be prevented. It uses the traffic light as symbol. "The idea is simple. We have clear No-Go limits – Reds, and marginal conditions – Ambers. If there are no problems we are in the clear – Green. We must always stop if we have a Red, but too many Ambers are just as risky. The rule says, Three Ambers = Red. When we have too many Ambers, we can try to manage some of them back to Green, maintaining control of what might become an escalating situation[1]." The point of the Rule of Three is that it helps employees gain situational awareness, they gain insight into how many problems there are and where the risks can accumulate.

We can also find examples of how this is done in healthcare. In 1981 William Knaus, then Associate Professor of Anesthesiology and Computer Medicine at the George Washington University Medical Center, introduced the APACHE score as a measure of the condition of patients on the ICU. The score is built up out of several parameters, including age, temperature, blood pressure, pH measurement, heart rate and kidney function. These are all separate risk factors brought together to create one comprehensive view of the patient's condition: accumulation of separate risks into one score. Research proved that the score had predictive value for both therapy effectiveness and survival. The APACHE score has been simplified over the years and is now used around the world in ICUs. The higher the score, the higher the expected mortality.

The so called rapid response system (RRS) works the same way. The idea behind RRS is that you identify and respond to patients with early signs of clinical deterioration before the patient actually suffers a respiratory or cardiac arrest. The first paediatric RRS was implemented in 2005 by James Tibballs and his colleagues at the Royal Children's Hospital in Melbourne, Australia². Research showed there are measurable parameters that can predict the chance of a heart attack. Interestingly, one of these parameters is gut feeling. Other parameters are heart rate, blood pressure, respiratory rate, temperature and conscious state. These are all dynamic parameters that each, by itself, would not be a reason for calling for help if they were only mildly abnormal. But taken together, these parameters create a pretty good prediction of what will happen to the patient if adequate care is not given at this stage. Although there is some discussion as to whether implementation of a RRS really reduces mortality and morbidity, it without doubt helps structure the assessment of a patient's condition and the subsequent communication. The patient is 'scored' as a whole, not as a series of subproblems that are underestimated or referred to various specialists. Before introduction of RRS, a raised heart rate could lead to paging a cardiologist, a patient with difficulty in breathing would be referred to a pulmonologist and a neurologist would be called if the patient developed a lowered conscious state. The RRS scoring system creates overview and a language with which a nurse can clearly communicate with a critical care specialist.

Let's get back to the gynaecologists, who honestly did not know what they could do differently to prevent a future similar unexpected outcome. They followed the guidelines for each problem they encountered, didn't they? A 41+ weeks pregnancy is no reason for a caesarean, low amniotic fluid volume is no reason for a caesarean, slow dilatation is no reason for a caesarean, meconium-stained liquor is no reason for a caesarean, CTG decelerations attributed to vena cauda syndrome are no reason for a caesarean. In summary, there was no reason to take action. In another situation a heart rate of 105 bpm, a systolic blood pressure of 100 mmHg, a slight tachypnoea and a worried nurse would each in itself not lead to the nurse to take action. Thanks to the RRS these separate entities are combined into one score. The comprehensive view this creates leads to the nurse recognising the portent of an adverse outcome and paging a doctor.

Accumulating the separate risks sets action into motion. Sometimes this action turns out to be unnecessary, sometimes it saves a patient's life.

The gynaecologists' reaction, the investigating committee's conclusions and the evaluation by the external expert are all understandable if viewed from their perspectives. However, their perspectives were limited. I do not claim to have expertise on obstetric risk factors and know myself to be nowhere near as knowledgeable as the gynaecologists concerned. I can't help noticing, however, that they limit their view to the separate risks and to the risk within their own specialist domain. If they had scored the separate risks and added them together, like other medical domains have learned to do, they would have probably decided to escalate the situation sooner.

That is the lesson I take from this case. Risks are not separate entities, they are a piece of the whole and should be viewed as such. Individual drops do not form a flood, but if enough drops fall into a bucket, at some point you only need one more drop for the bucket to spill. At that point you are too late and overtaken by events. In Chapter 7 I gave an example of non-technical risks that could be scored, the Nine Red Flags, that seem applicable for all medical professions. Bram's case teaches me that it seems useful also to identify risks specific for certain medical domains and create a system that helps you accumulate these risks, like the APACHE and RRS scores do. Especially when you are caught up in an acute situation, or, as in Bram's case, you are up to your ears in the situation for several days, it is predictable that you lose sight of the bigger picture. That is when you need a system to help remind you which risks have accumulated so far, how many Ambers you've collected, how full the bucket has become. Then you can anticipate how many extra risks are still acceptable before it is time to escalate, before the bucket suddenly spills.

HOW CAN THIS HELP ME TODAY?

Do not weigh risk factors in a patient's care path separately, but write them down and add them up.

HOW CAN I INVOLVE MY PATIENTS?

Explain to the patient which criteria you will use in your decision to escalate, so the patient can help you be alert when these occur. This way you can make escalation of care, where possible, a mutual decision.

CHAPTER 11
A just culture

THE CASE

Sometimes the dice seem to roll just right. Because my husband Spencer was off to a meeting, I had to take the kids to day-care and therefore took the car to work. It was beautiful weather outside and I would have certainly gone by bike to work otherwise. And then I would have had to cycle through the drizzle to the other location in the afternoon. I was nearing the end of my fourth year of the General Surgery rotation. In the morning Greg Wilson, one of the surgeons, had asked me if I could take over for him in the other location of the hospital that afternoon. He emailed me the list of patients to be operated on. Two inguinal hernias, a lipoma, an ingrown toenail and a carpal tunnel. I had heaps of experience in all of these procedures, so I felt comfortable enough to fill in for Greg.

"No problem," I replied. I had been assigned as an extra on the A&E that afternoon but it wasn't that busy so my colleague could manage without me.

It was a bit of a nuisance that the hospital had two locations, on the other hand it provided a nice break in the day to travel from one to the other. I was looking forward to the procedures. Pretty straightforward, no one looking over my shoulder, friendly nurses, just enjoying doing my own thing. It certainly beat hanging around the A&E forced to listen to ambulance crews dishing out boring sports trivia. I caught myself grinning as I walked to the car park.

The procedures went well. The last patient was a Mr Zobieda, a 48-year-old Syrian immigrant with CTS. The clerks couldn't find his chart. It was probably in the main hospital location, as so often happened. Our hospital at that time did not have an electronic patient record and charts were transported between the two locations by a courier. Unpractical and prone to mistakes, as we saw once again today. But anyway, CTS was not rocket science and the patient was reasonably able to express himself in his broken English.

"Is it this hand, Mr Zobieda?" I asked as I took his right hand.

"Yes Doctor, ai ai, pain here," and he pointed his left index finger to the hand I was holding. "Using hammer no good, hurts, doctor."

67

A carpal tunnel decompression procedure is pretty easy. You make a single cut in the wrist, find the carpal ligament and cut it. This reduces the pressure on the median nerve in the wrist. Easy does it. So I went through the steps, stitched him up neatly and jotted down a brief operative report. I drove back to the main location for the afternoon handover. Nothing extraordinary had occurred, so I could actually leave the hospital with plenty of time for once to pick up the girls at day-care. Sometimes the dice seem to roll just right.

Two weeks later Greg Wilson paged me.

"Stephany, what on God's green earth is wrong with you? You performed the wrong bloody procedure!"

My heart skipped a beat. What was he talking about, which procedure? In my mind I ran through all the procedures I had performed the past few days.

"What… what are you talking about, Greg? Which patient do you mean?"

"Mr Zobieda, the Syrian carpenter you operated on at the outpatient clinic. You treated him for CTS in his right hand. But he didn't have CTS, he has Quervain. You performed the wrong procedure on him. Seriously, what were you thinking?"

I couldn't understand it. How could I have botched this up? I was certain Greg had emailed me the list of procedures himself and I had definitely read CTS on that list. I shook my head. Unbelievable. But Greg had been pretty adamant on the phone, and very cross. I opened my mailbox and retrieved Greg's email from my deleted items. And the list was exactly as I remembered it: two inguinal hernias, a lipoma, an ingrown toenail and a carpal tunnel. Thank God, I thought, at least I'm not crazy. But that was of no help to the patient. He had undergone the wrong procedure and now had to have surgery a second time.

The next day I went to the out-patient clinic to try and find out how it had happened. I soon discovered a sequence of unfortunate events. Mr Zobieda was so impaired by his right hand, that he wasn't able to work as carpenter. This meant he had no income. An orthopaedic surgeon had diagnosed his complaints as De Quervain's tendonitis and added the patient to his waiting list. Cindy, who managed the bookings, had spoken with Mr Zobieda briefly and sympathised with him. She asked her colleague Olivia to help find a spot higher up on the waiting list. Olivia looked at the chart and asked Cindy which procedure was performed for a De Quervain's tendonitis.

"They slice through the ligament," Cindy had replied. "Oh, in that case the patient doesn't have to be seen by an orthopaedic surgeon, the general surgeons also do carpal tunnel. Let's see. Here, Dr Wilson has a free spot next week. Let's add Mr Zobieda to his list."

Without consulting the clinicians, the medical secretaries had placed the patient on another list, all with good intent. And in the process they had unwittingly changed the diagnosis. Same procedure alright, cutting through a ligament. Only it's a different ligament. This chain of events also explained the missing chart. A surgical chart had never been made, only an orthopaedic chart. And orthopaedic charts are never sent along if a patient is referred to another speciality.

I shared my findings with Greg Wilson and he shook his head.

"What a mess. Well, I'm sorry Steph, I should never have reacted to you the way I did." And that was that, we both went back to work.

REFLECTION

All people concerned had acted with the best intentions for the patient. The ladies of administration had felt bad for the patient for having to wait so long for his treatment and went out of their way to expedite his operation. The surgeon wanted to prevent having to cancel the afternoon procedures and found a replacement so his patients would not have their treatment postponed. The junior surgeon wanted to help out, and organised that she would not be missed at the A&E Department. Everybody did their utmost to help the patient and that's when it got messed up.

Sadly I have seen this happen many times, a doctor filling in for a colleague and subsequently becoming involved in an adverse outcome. An ophthalmologist stepping in to help out a colleague and then operating on the wrong eye. A patient left incontinent after surgery because gynaecologist A had prepared for the procedure but dropped out, gynaecologist B who took over was called off to an emergency procedure and then gynaecologist C stepped in, with the best intentions but without an adequate handover. Crucial information about the patient's abnormal anatomy and the specifics of the planned procedure was lost. Gynaecologist C expected a routine operation and the procedure was well underway before he realised that the situation transcended his competencies. By then the irreparable damage to the patient's urinary tract had already been done.

Healthcare professionals often cover for one another, out of collegiality and out of empathy for the patient. I urge you to keep doing this. What you might not always realise, at that moment, is that your chances of becoming involved in an adverse event are higher than normal. There is an extra handover, which increases the chance of information loss. But also, and maybe that is the heart of the problem, so called 'tacit knowledge' gets lost. Tacit knowledge is the kind of knowledge that is difficult to transfer to another person by means of writing it down or verbalising it, because it's not explicit and you might even be unaware that you have it. The doctor who had originally prepared to treat the patient had made a mental model of the patient that is only partly possible to hand over. The doctor who steps in has not had time to process all the information to create a similarly thorough mental model, so this doctor creates his or her own one, which might not always be similar to the original doctor's. As when gynaecologist C's expectation of the patient did not coincide with gynaecologist A's in the example above. So if you are covering for a colleague, be aware that you run a higher chance of making mistakes.

I want to use this case to highlight another theme that cannot be missed in this book: 'a just culture'. The first reaction of surgeon Greg Wilson, when he hears Stephany has performed the wrong procedure, is to blame her for it. "What on God's green earth is wrong with you?" and "What were you thinking?" are accusations. They express a value judgement, and quite a negative one at that. Surgeon Wilson based his judgement on the outcome, on the fact that the patient had undergone the wrong procedure. Because something went wrong, we automatically infer that the person involved must have screwed up. The larger the damage, the larger the screw-up. This is even engrained in our judicial system. If you drive through a red light you get a fine, if you run a red light and kill a pedestrian, you go to jail. The punishment is based on the outcome. This might be acceptable from a standpoint of retribution (what happened is really bad, so the punishment must be likewise), although I do not share that view, but from a safety standpoint it is downright counterproductive. This policy leads to people putting their energy into hiding bad outcomes instead of using adverse outcomes to learn and improve. Fate has a considerable influence on outcome. In all the cases I described in the preceding chapters, you can imagine that the outcome would have been different if the cards had been dealt differently. Fate befalls us, it is not something we can influence. We can, however, influence behavioural choices and the factors prompting these choices. These aspects offer opportunities for us to influence the preconditions for creating safer healthcare. So focussing on behaviour instead of on outcome offers more opportunities to actually improve healthcare. An added benefit of such a policy, is that it gives more justice to the healthcare professionals involved. It is more fair to judge somebody's role in an adverse outcome on that person's behavioural choices and the factors prompting those choices, than on the severity of the outcome. Shifting the focus from outcome to behaviour is in the heart of a 'just culture'.

In the case of Mr Zobieda, Stephany was judged by her supervising surgeon and he judged her based on the adverse outcome. Later on, when it turned out not to be her fault, he apologised. That was a gracious gesture, but too late. What he should have done is suspend his judgement on Stephany until he had enough information to understand the circumstances in which she had made the mistake. That would have lowered the bar for Stephany to be open about future mistakes, which would have benefited her surgical training. One of the 'founding fathers' of the patient safety movement, Dr Lucian Leape, repeatedly stressed that a punitive work environment and the widely held belief that errors are evidence of personal carelessness push many healthcare workers into reporting only what they cannot conceal: "The single greatest impediment to error prevention is that we punish people for making mistakes[1]." People do not choose to make mistakes or become involved in adverse outcomes. Even though I have been interested in the concept of a just culture for many years and passionately believe it is better not to judge a person on based on outcome alone, I still get it wrong all too often. I can't find the car keys and my reflex is to assume my wife has left them in the wrong spot. My child spills her glass of milk, so I immediately assume she has been messing around. The more milk she spills, the angrier I get. A car overtakes me, switches to my lane and then decelerates so I scold the driver for not paying attention. It is so incredibly hard to suppress this instinctive reflex and look at an adverse outcome with an open mind and without value judgements. But if you want to learn from stuff that goes wrong, it is essential to get that right. I realise this as a friend, a father, a husband and as a healthcare inspector.

In all of the chapters in this book I describe how healthcare professionals become involved in unintended adverse outcomes. You could say they made mistakes. Stephany performed the wrong procedure, the obstetricians misjudged the patient's risks, the GPs missed the meningitis, etcetera. But the reader will have noticed that I never fix the blame. I don't deny the severity of the situations, they are mostly dramatic, but I don't believe fixing the blame will help prevent future recurrence of similar incidents. It just doesn't help. I untangle the two elements, outcome and behaviour, and then try to understand the behaviour within the context at that moment in time. Understanding behaviour offers handles for adapting the circumstances to facilitate the right behaviour in future situations. This helps decrease the chances of adverse outcomes and thus improves healthcare safety. Sometimes you discover that behaviour was blameworthy, I will get back to that later on in this chapter, but in the past 15 years I have learned that my gut feeling to blame somebody seldom turns out to be justified. Investigation into the context always leads to a much more balanced view. A healthcare professional rarely harms a patient on purpose. It is much more common to do your best for a patient and then unintentionally become involved in harming that patient. James Reason, the English psychologist who coined the 'Swiss Cheese Model', developed a culpability model to guide the assessment of an individual's role in an adverse outcome[2]. The NHS National Patient Safety Agency in England translated this model to healthcare and called it an 'incident decision tree' (**Figure 11.1**). You can find plenty of information about this tool on the internet. The tool comprises an algorithm and poses a series of structured questions to help managers decide which action towards the employee involved is most appropriate. Basically it consists of four types of question:

- Was the harm intended?
- Was the employee incapacitated in any way (e.g. depression, drugs)?
- Did the employee adhere to protocols and safe working practices and were these adequate and available?
- Would somebody with the same background act the same in a similar situation?

The Dutch gynaecologist Martijn Heringa used the incident decision tree in 2008 to assess 40 incidents that had been reported within his department. His conclusion was that not one of these incidents justified action towards the healthcare professional involved. This was contrary to the professionals' first reaction. Dr Heringa wrote: "They often think they themselves, or others, are responsible or even guilty. Using the incident decision tree helps deal with the individuals in a more just manner, creating more faith in the safety of the organization".[3]

From a safety perspective, the most important issue after an adverse event, besides mitigating its effects, is preventing recurrence of similar events. This requires insight into the root causes. Because a large part of healthcare is created by human actions, as opposed to machines, an investigator will be dependent

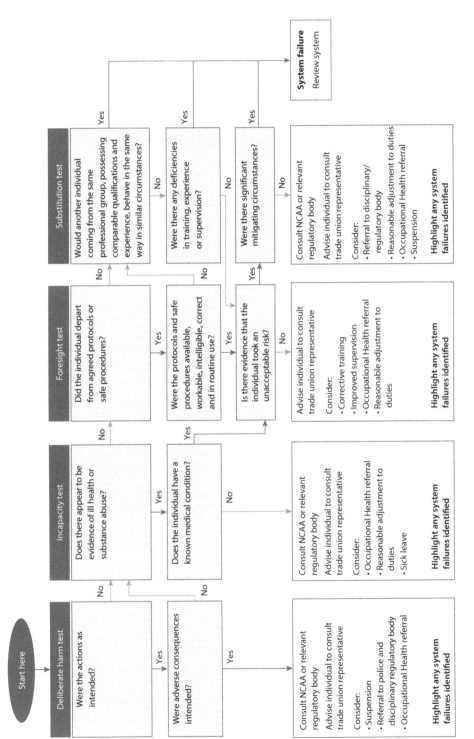

Figure 11.1 Incident decision tree.

upon humans to gather the required information for analysis. You can hardly expect people to be open and honest if they do not know how their role will be judged and what consequences the outcome of the investigation could have for them personally. Using the incident decision tree can help clarify this for all involved. However, it is just a tool. Understanding the fundamental principles behind this tool is much more important.

A book that really helped me understand the principles behind a just culture is *Whack-a-Mole* by David Marx[4]. Throughout the book, he makes the argument that there are two inputs impacting on our ability to avoid adverse events: the design of the system and the behavioural choices of the people within those systems. He describes three types of behaviour: normal, at-risk and reckless behaviour. Risky behaviour occurs when the person is not aware of the risk, or has made a deliberate choice to accept the risk in light of the expected benefit. With reckless behaviour the risk is taken consciously and cannot be justified by the expected benefit, for example driving at twice the speed limit through the city centre to get home on time for dinner. You hardly ever encounter reckless behaviour at the workplace, because it's simply not worth it. Marx suggests a simple model:

- Console the human error.
- Coach the at-risk behaviour.
- Punish the reckless behaviour. Independent of the outcome.

I would like to add to this: stimulate normal behaviour and reward exemplary behaviour, independent of the outcome.

'Independent of the outcome' was a real eye-opener for me. So if something went well, but the person doing it acted recklessly while doing it, he or she should be punished for the behaviour. This is, however strange it might sound, just. Because you implicitly reward those who abide by the expected behavioural norms and you strengthen those norms. The difficulty lies in drawing the line between risky and reckless. This is seldom a clear line, but usually more like a grey area.

Sidney Dekker highlights this grey area in his work. In his book *Just Culture* he gives various examples, inside and outside of healthcare, of people who were involved in an adverse outcome and were punished for their role[5]. Dekker claims the judicial system of today has many hallmarks of the witch hunts in the Middle Ages. Sentences are based on outcome and the interpretation of the events prior to the adverse outcome is highly biased by knowledge of the outcome. He argues that it is essential for a safety culture for people to know where the line is between acceptable and unacceptable behaviour, between risky and reckless, and, even more important, who draws this line. The 'grey area' needs to be as small as possible. For this, three elements need to be present: an independent judge, a jury of peers and the right to appeal. When these are present, a person involved in an adverse outcome can trust that his or her contribution to that outcome will be judged fairly. In later work, Dekker describes what he calls 'Just Culture 2.0'.

This, he explains, is not focussed on a just way to handle the professionals involved in an adverse event, but on the needs of the victims after the event. He calls this 'restorative justice', as opposed to 'retributive justice'. This discussion goes beyond the scope of this book and, if you are interested, I recommend Dekker's work. The point I want to make here is that people need to know how and by whom they will be judged, if you expect them to be open about their own mistakes.

There is one last aspect I want to highlight from Stephany's case: behavioural norms shift over time. This case took place many years ago, before the presurgical time-out had become mainstream. Nowadays, in many countries, the procedure would not have taken place because the presurgical time-out could not have been performed properly without the patient's chart present. So if exactly the same situation took place today, Stephany's behaviour would have been blameworthy because choosing to neglect the time-out procedure is considered reckless behaviour. Ten years ago it was normal, 5 years ago it would be considered risky to start without an adequate time-out and since it has been implemented widely and mandated by accreditation and regulatory authorities, it is considered reckless not to adhere to the time-out procedure. In these countries, all surgeons are aware of the time-out procedure, hospitals have had enough time to implement the procedure and the procedure has been integrated into operating theatre processes. The choice to adhere to the time-out procedure has been placed outside the individual doctor's autonomy, just like the choice to smoke in the operating theatre. I can only speak for the Netherlands, but if a surgeon now neglects the time-out procedure, he or she will be held accountable for this choice. Independent of the outcome.

Society is constantly changing and our behavioural norms change too. Not wearing seatbelts, smoking in public spaces, driving under the influence are all examples of behaviour that was acceptable or even normal 40 years ago. I remember in my own youth how my father could fit seven of my teammates in one vehicle, by stuffing a couple in the boot. And we loved riding in the boot. That would be totally unacceptable in my country today. Our norms shift and the rules and laws are adjusted accordingly. This happens in society, and, just as much, in healthcare. So the line between risky and reckless behaviour is not just a grey area, it also shifts over time. That makes it all the more important to make clear rules on where the line is and who gets to define the boundaries when push comes to shove.

You don't always have influence on how others judge your actions. You do have influence on how you judge the actions of others. By being an example you can inspire the people around you and contribute to creating a just culture. The first step is to be aware of the ingrained human reflex to base one's conclusion on the outcome of events. Make an effort to suppress this reflex and look at facts and circumstances with an open mind. Then try to draw a fair conclusion on the behaviour prior to the outcome, by for instance asking the question: "Is it likely somebody else would have done the same in similar circumstances?" And if so, what can be changed so as to prompt the right choices or behaviour in the future? Don't fix the blame, fix the problem.

HOW CAN THIS HELP ME TODAY?

- Be aware that 'stepping in' for a colleague creates an extra risk of making mistakes.
- Everybody makes mistakes. Do not base your judgement of people on the outcome, but on their behaviour within the context of that point in time. Praise exemplary behaviour, stimulate normal behaviour, coach risky behaviour and never accept reckless behaviour, independent of the outcome.

HOW CAN I INVOLVE MY PATIENTS?

When you step in for a colleague, make sure you take a thorough history yourself. "I realise you have already told my colleague all about it. I spoke to him/her and I have also read your file. But I want to go over it with you one more time, just to be sure that I have understood all the information correctly."

CHAPTER 12
Blind faith

THE CASE

My son Josh had helped me find a suitable nursing home. He had taken leave from work to visit different locations, the dear. Eventually he suggested I should choose Cloverfield Convalescence and Nursing Home to recover from my hip replacement surgery. It had a cosy dining room with a lovely view over the rolling countryside hills, Josh said. The rooms were tidy and relatively spacious. I had hardly nodded my head before Josh paced to the nurses' station to organise that my postoperative transfer would be set in motion. Fortunately they had room, and so it transpired that I was transferred to Cloverfield Convalescence and Nursing Home 2 days after my surgery.

I was welcomed by a very sweet nurse who helped Josh store my things in my room. When this was done, she walked me to Dr O'Brian. I handed him the hospital's referral letter. He scanned it and looked at me.

"Excellent, I read here that the procedure was successfully completed without any complications. The ward nurse writes that your wound looks good. That's great news. How are you feeling today, Mrs Callaghan?"

"I feel fine, Doctor, thank you. It's all going better than I expected."

"Good. Good. I expect you must be tired from the journey here. We'll keep it brief so you can enjoy a cup of coffee in a moment. Let's take a look at your medication." He read aloud the medications in the referral letter and checked if I used them. It was all correct. Josh ran the medications by a list he appeared to have drawn up earlier. He also confirmed that the medications were correct.

"Great, that's that then. Let's see, I will order the nurse to inspect your wound on a daily basis and consult with the wound care sister if needed. Just let me print this out and then we're all set. Good." Doctor O'Brian swivelled in his chair to fish a piece of paper out of the printer, perforated two holes in it and inserted the paper in a blue binder that lay on his desk. He clapped the binder shut, stepped out from behind his table and handed the binder to Josh.

"If you would be so kind as to escort your mother to her room and hand this chart to the nurse. Great, much appreciated. Mrs Callaghan, I wish you a pleasant stay with us and will see you again soon." He shook both our hands and held the door for us.

Later that day, in the afternoon, my leg started to feel sore. It hurt a little and it felt swollen. The nurse came around to take a look. She examined both my legs and reassured me.

"I think it's nothing to worry about, Mrs. Callaghan. Maybe your leg feels a wee irritated because you have been sitting a lot today. You know what, why don't I raise the footrest? Here, that should be nice and comfy. Please don't hesitate to let me know if this doesn't help. Is there anything else I can do, can I maybe fetch you a cup of tea, Mrs Callaghan?"

The first couple of days passed by without anything notable happening. I met some nice people and enjoyed myself playing cards and resting in the spring sunshine. Each morning, while she washed me, the nurse checked on my surgical wound. I noticed the bandages were always a bit moist, light red with a yellowish streak in the middle. The wound itself remained reddish. I didn't like the look of it, a long red scar with a row of staples in it. After a week a new nurse came to check the wound. She introduced herself as Cassidy Flynn, wound care nurse.

"I was told your wound was still leaking a little. Could I take a look, Mrs. Callaghan?" Cassidy removed the dressing an inspected my wound. "Hmm, the wound is still a little bit open. It doesn't seem infected however. Well, Mrs Callaghan, I don't see any reason for concern. I will make a note for the nurses."

Doctor O'Brian visited me in my room on Monday. I had raised my concerns about my leg with nurse Nora. My leg didn't feel right, it hurt. I was also concerned about my wound not healing properly. Dr O'Brian made some changes in my medication so the pain would be less of a nuisance. He did not look at my wound and it had not occurred to me to ask him to. Besides, the poor man was clearly overloaded with work.

Cassidy Flynn, the wound care nurse, returned on Tuesday. She removed the bandage and inspected my wound thoroughly. Then she removed the staples with some sort of special tweezers. Cassidy told me she didn't think the wound had changed much since she last saw me. I found it strange that there was still fluid seeping out. By chance Josh was present and he asked Cassidy if this was normal, if the doctor should see it, if I shouldn't be prescribed antibiotics. He's a sweet boy, but quite the worrying type sometimes. Cassidy reassured us. As far as she was concerned, it was all going as expected and if we remained concerned it would be no trouble for her at all to come back to me.

The next day the dressing had to be replaced for the second time in the afternoon, because wound fluids had leaked right through. The nurse dabbed the wound with iodine and applied clean dressing. She also measured my temperature by poking a device in my ear. I did not have a fever.

Josh visited me after work on Thursday. When he asked, I told him the wound was still quite tender. This worried him. He insisted the nurse contact the hospital to inquire if this was normal. They were attentive at Cloverfield because they made the call immediately.

"We called the orthopaedic ward you were admitted to," nurse Nora told us, "and there is no cause for concern. We agreed we would call them again tomorrow if anything changes in your condition."

But the following afternoon the wound really start to hurt. It also felt warmer than before. Cassidy came by promptly and fetched Dr O'Brian. The wound was oozing even more yellowish fluid than the previous days. It looked quite unpleasant to me. Dr O'Brian was also clearly alarmed. He consulted with the hospital and set up my transfer so the orthopaedic surgeon could evaluate the situation himself. I asked Nora to call Josh for me.

In the hospital I was readmitted to the same ward as before. The orthopaedic surgeon told me that the wound was infected. I was administered antibiotics and on Saturday morning they performed a revision. When I woke up, I was told they had had to remove the prosthesis and replace it. The previous prosthesis had been infected. It took 2 weeks before I could leave the hospital. Josh organised my transfer to a different care home, as we had lost our confidence in Cloverfield. They had clearly failed in recognising my hip infection on time.

For 3 months I had to take those terrible antibiotics. I think I was nauseous the whole time. Dreadful, you just cannot imagine. When all had passed I came to realise how inadequate my care had been at Cloverfield. I returned with Josh to state my complaints. The manager would take our complaints into consideration. When we had not heard back from him after a month, we lodged an official complaint.

REFLECTION

Mrs Callaghan's complaint led to an internal review. The review committee concluded that Dr O'Brian had disregarded his responsibility by not examining the postoperative wound himself during the intake. He had trusted completely on the paper handover provided to him by the hospital. He had not performed any form of physical examination at all. The committee deemed this a key contributing factor to the delay in recognising the patient's wound infection.

So the lesson from this case is: never blindly trust information you are given about a patient that is referred to you. We regularly receive incident reports at the Healthcare Inspectorate I work for, describing situations in which a doctor heedlessly accepts a diagnosis made by a previous doctor without verifying this with his or her own observation. This leads to wounds being underestimated, pressure ulcers overlooked, malnutrition or dehydration missed, needless interventions performed or critical treatments withheld. In Mrs Callaghan's case, the diagnosis of postoperative wound infection was delayed, impairing the orthopaedic surgeon in his treatment possibilities. Maybe an earlier detection would also have led to surgical revision, those things are always hard to tell. What is abundantly clear, however, is that the level of care provided by Cloverfield was below the level they had intended and below the level Mrs Callaghan needed. Never blindly trust information you are given about a patient that is referred to you. But is it really that simple?

Dr O'Brian, who had over 10 years of experience in nursing homes, told the review committee he was well aware that a physical examination should be an integral part of every intake. He had omitted the physical because he thought it would be too taxing for Mrs Callaghan, as she had already had such a demanding day. He added to this that he regularly skipped the physical due to lack of time. They had been understaffed for 4 years already. Although on paper the nursing home had four full-time physicians employed, in fact there were only three, one of which was a physician assistant. Of these three, two worked part-time. Dr O'Brian had raised his concerns about this situation several times over the past years, both to the manager and directly to the board. They kept telling him it was out of their control, as they were not able to find doctors to fill the vacancies. There were just not enough nursing home doctors out there. Dr O'Brian and his colleagues worked around the clock to keep the home running. He explicitly did not mention all this as a justification for missing the wound infection. No, he felt terrible for missing it and it pained him that he had let Mrs Callaghan down. He described his situation to give the committee some feeling for the context prompting his mistake.

Work pressure almost always leads to a focus on efficiency, and consequently to safety compromises. The Danish safety scientist Erik Hollnagel calls this the 'ETTO principle', ETTO standing for Efficiency–Thoroughness Trade-Off: "People are expected to be both efficient and thorough at the same time – or rather to be thorough, when with hindsight it was wrong to be efficient[1]." The hindsight he refers to is a large pitfall for me as healthcare inspector. I only see the cases where trusting a colleague has led to an adverse outcome. My gut reaction in those cases is: "Why didn't the doctor just do the physical, like he/she was supposed to? What is wrong with this doctor?" However, I do not see the countless cases in which skipping the physical examination did not lead to a negative outcome and created time for the doctor to solve other problems that otherwise might have led to adverse outcomes. For Dr O'Brian it was efficient, and in some way client centred, not to perform the physical at that point in time. He was well aware he was omitting something he was supposed to do. When it turned out this led to missing a wound infection, he was held accountable. The question is: how well aware was he really at the time? Was the trade-off that he made justifiable, with the knowledge he had at that time?

We all make trade-offs on a daily basis. Eating tasty but unhealthy food, playing sports despite the chance of injuries, yielding to a nagging child despite knowing this will turn against you later, writing a text a little sloppier to finish on time. Without trade-offs we would grind to a halt. But every trade-off creates the risk of unconsciously accepting further trade-offs, further concessions. When the trade-off pertains to safety, this can become dangerous. Adverse events do not occur often, so trade-offs on safety can seem justifiable as long as nothing bad happens. This is a well-known phenomenon in safety science and is called 'normalisation of deviance'. Diane Vaughan, professor at Columbia University's Department of

Sociology, developed the theory of the normalisation of deviance in her book *The Challenger Launch Decision*[2]. She describes how, during the developmental phase of the Space Shuttle Programme, the normalisation of deviance resulted in a dangerous design flaw in the design of the spacecraft. She says: "Normalization of deviance means that people within the organization become so much accustomed to a deviant behavior that they don't consider it as deviant, despite the fact that they far exceed their own rules for the elementary safety." Little steps take you slowly but surely into a situation that is far less safe then you wished. You skip the physical examination of a new patient just this once due to lack of time and it turns out nothing goes wrong. You have now unwittingly lowered your threshold for skipping a physical examination. The more often you skip it, the easier it becomes and the less bad you feel about it. It never leads to any patient harm, so all's well. Until one day, skipping the physical has inconspicuously become normal to you. At that moment, it's just a matter of time before you're hit in the face by an adverse event. And then you rediscover the reason why the physical examination had always been an integral part of every new patient's intake.

Trade-offs are related to values. You weigh one value (e.g. efficiency) in relation to another value (e.g. thoroughness). Values are rooted in cultural norms or even laid down in the law to prevent people making trade-offs society deems unacceptable (driving too fast, robbing somebody to make money). Most of us instinctively sense it when we are crossing a normative boundary, when we are making an unacceptable trade-off. Dr O'Brian was well aware that a physical examination should be an integral part of every intake. He had felt uneasy about his choice to skip it with Mrs Callaghan. How we judge his decision is influenced by the value we place on a physical examination, or, to take it one step further: by the value we place on a doctor always examining his or her own patients. Is this an absolute norm, or are there circumstances imaginable where the doctor can deviate from this norm, and if so, was Dr O'Brian in such a circumstance? Is it black and white, or are there grey areas? People will differ in their opinions on this.

My opinion is that a doctor should possess enough information to be able to autonomously propose the best treatment options to his or her patient. The information does not have to be complete, it seldom is, but rich enough to allow the doctor to make a considered treatment proposal to the patient. I consider this a fundamental precondition for bearing the responsibility for the doctor's part in any doctor–patient relationship. I expect Dr O'Brian did not have insight into the expertise of the hospital's ward nurse who wrote Mrs Callaghan's handover. I mean no disrespect to the nurse, but I feel this anonymous source of information alone was insufficient for Dr O'Brian to make a considered treatment proposal. That trade-off, bluntly put 'betting the handover is correct to save time', feels to me like breaching the duty of care, irrespective of the outcome, so also if Mrs Callaghan had not suffered a wound infection. Dr O'Brian and his colleagues have over the years come to accept a situation in which they were not able to fulfil their duty of care. He raised the issue, several times even, but by accepting the situation also perpetuated it. Undoubtedly with the best intentions for his patients, but nevertheless resulting in his patients receiving substandard care.

All things considered, I maintain what I wrote at the beginning of this reflection. The lesson from this case is: never blindly trust information you are given about a patient that is referred to you. Always make sure that you are able, of your own accord, to propose the best treatment options to your patient. If you are not able to, for whatever reason, you should not accept the referral because this increases the chances of an adverse outcome for the patient.

HOW CAN THIS HELP ME TODAY?

Never blindly trust information you are given about a patient who is referred to you. Make your own assessment of the patient's condition.

HOW CAN I INVOLVE MY PATIENTS?

Explain to your patient that you might repeat questions that have already been asked or repeat examinations that have already been performed. You understand that this might be inconvenient for the patient or create the impression that you have not read the chart or the referral letter. This is not the case. You are doing this to make sure you understand the information correctly, so you can provide the best possible care for the patient.

CHAPTER 13
Bias

THE CASE

This may sound strange, but I am glad the newspaper has decided to publish our story. We deeply want the whole story to become known. Other parents might learn from our experiences. And certainly other doctors can. Even though it's still tough for us to talk about what happened, especially when you consider how it all could have turned out. I want to share what Rachel and I went through, preferably on television too one day. If this can in any way help prevent others having to suffer through the same ordeal, it's worth it.

A relieved father.

Can you tell me how it all started?

Rachel was three and a half when we took her to the hospital for the first time. No, actually, it started even earlier. I must tell you that I have had some trouble walking and speaking for ages. People often think I'm drunk. Yeah, I'll enjoy a beer or two on occasions, but never during the day. Okay, nearly never. The point is, that I always talk like this, even when I'm completely sober. There's nothing I can do about it. It's because I have ADCA, you know. The doctor diagnosed me. Said this made me disabled and so I've been declared unfit for work. Basically the doctor said I'm not allowed to work anymore. For years now. I had a job before, you know. After primary school I went to work at my uncle's, in farming. Uncle Winston, he was like a second dad to me. But the work was tough for me. And the headaches I would get, just unbearable. When that happened, I couldn't do any work. But Uncle Winston understood, he never called me liar or anything like that.

We were discussing your daughter, Rachel. You went to the hospital with her. What did they find?

Yeah, that's what I'm saying. I was in the front garden. I clearly remember because the night before we had lost to Argentina, so we were out of the World Championships.

83

But our boys had stood their ground, if you ask me, but Argentina had more luck. We had decorated the whole neighbourhood in the colours of our national team so now I was taking down the flag banners from the fence. Suddenly I hear a terrible scream. So I go into the room and find Rachel on the ground next to her little table. She was grabbing her head and screaming like she was going to die. I was terrified. She was inconsolable, like she didn't even see or hear I was there. So I panicked, you know. What would you do? I called 999. Could hardly make myself clear to the lady on the phone, but she hears Rachel screaming in the background and gets the picture. So here comes the ambulance. We get in, and they take us to the hospital. By now Rachel is doing a little better, she's stopped screaming. We get to see a doctor. So I tell him about me taking down the flag banners and the sudden screaming inside the house. The doctor goes to fetch a nurse and together they examine Rachel. They ask her to walk some, which she does okay. I help undress Rachel and the doctor examines her further. Rachel has a small wound on her head. I tell the doctor I think maybe she fell against the side of the table. I wasn't there, I was outside, you know. The other bruises, Doctor? You tell me. Kids play, kids fall, they get bruises I guess. And I go on to tell the doctor about my own problems walking. It's because of the ADCA. I want to explain but the doctor has little attention for me, only seems interested in Rachel. Which I get, because she's the reason we're in the hospital. The doctor couldn't find anything. He gave Rachel something for the pain and we we're off again.

And after that?

Well, a couple of months later I was horsing around with Rachel. It was on a Wednesday afternoon, Rachel had been going to preschool for some weeks. We were wrestling on the bed when she fell off. Clumsy of me, right, but I didn't mean her to fall off. Rachel falls on the ground and starts screaming again like a butchered pig. Just like the time during the World Cup. She grabs her head and throws up, vomits all over the floor and herself. So I call 999 again. The paramedics carry her into the ambulance this time, because Rachel is all dazed. We get to the hospital and the same things happen. The doc examines her but finds nothing out of the ordinary. Asks me like three times what exactly happened and if anybody else was in the house when it happened. No I say, because the wife was at work. He asks about the last time this happened, clearly he's reading about this on the computer screen. He also asks if I had been drinking. No, I say, and tell him about the ADCA and how my Uncle Winston never let me down despite not being able to work as hard as I wished I could. I kind of get the idea that doctors ask, but don't listen. Probably too busy or something. Anyway, end of the story is we go home again, just like last time.

Had you noticed anything different in Rachel, in between those two visits?

Well, her mother Michelle and I both have migraine. Rachel complained about headaches too now and again. How often, I don't remember. But she could be quite annoying for a couple of days then. Slow, weepy, not interested in doing anything much. The preschool teacher had asked us about this once. We thought Rachel had trouble adapting to school. So many new kids around her, all this new stuff. The teacher had approached Michelle about it, in a very lousy way. Like we were bad parents, like we were hiding something. Michelle was upset about it for a few days. Not good. But that's just how Rachel is, she can get cranky and then there's just nothing you can do but sit it out. Besides those moments she's a great kid. Really. And no matter how difficult she is, she'll always be the love of our life, our sweet little Rachel.

But then the situation really turned sour?

Yeah, a freaking nightmare. It was the third time we went to the hospital. Rachel had fallen again, screamed, clutched her head but only with her right hand. Her left arm and leg stayed still, she couldn't move them. It was heart breaking. I cried and panicked when I saw. It still moves me to talk about it now, sorry. We were seen by Dr Barth, I will never forget his name nor his face. A sturdy bloke with a big head of curly dark brown hair. He kind of looked like one of my mates. Dr Barth told us they were admitting Rachel to observe her a few days. I was relieved, but that turned out to be false. A nurse came to ask if I'd call my wife, because Dr Barth wanted to speak to both of us together. Well, what happened next is hard to describe. I'm still shocked when I think back to that moment. So when we sat there, across the desk from Dr Barth, he told us... how did he say it ... he suspected us of child abuse. He could find no other explanation for Rachel's symptoms. He had reported his suspicions to the authorities because he had to by law. It was out of his hands, the authorities would investigate this further. He and his team would focus on Rachel's wellbeing while she was in the hospital. I admit I can't remember the whole conversation. I kind of zoned out, I suppose, after he had mentioned child abuse. I was in utter shock. This was the worst thing that had ever happened to me, by far. For two nights Michelle and I lay awake at home anxiously, while the love of our life was surrounded by strangers in the hospital who thought we, of all people, had hurt her. And some unknown civil servant or something was out talking about us with the preschool teacher and God knows who.

And was that the moment they discovered your daughter had familial hemiplegic migraine?

Yes. We got a call from the hospital on Thursday morning. There had been another doctor, a neurologist if I remember correctly, who had wanted to do DNA testing. She had examined Rachel's case and told us she might be suffering from a genetic condition that caused her symptoms. That it might be possible I had the same condition. She asked our permission to do DNA tests. Of course we gave her our permission. We knew Rachel wasn't abused by us, we knew something else must be causing her headaches and falls. I had seen her fall myself and seen with my own eyes how much pain she was in afterwards. Apparently this new doctor had made her case convincingly, because Rachel was allowed to come home while we awaited the results of the DNA test. We're both forever grateful to her. And after 8 weeks we were told the result: Rachel had FHM. They also tested me and I have it too. It turns out I don't have ADCA, but FHM. What a relief! You see, the migraines you get because of FHM are more or less treatable. Since Rachel and I have started on medicines, we both have many fewer headaches. Rachel, knock on wood, hasn't had one attack yet like she had before. And she's doing a lot better at school too. We are so glad and grateful that the last doctor took us seriously and discovered the condition Rachel suffered from.

REFLECTION

It's every doctor's nightmare: missing an important diagnosis leading to your patient receiving essential treatment too late or not at all. Or, as in the case above, leading to wrongfully accusing parents of abusing their child. The paediatrician in this case, Dr Barth, was deeply upset by what had happened and wished he could turn back time. I don't think there is a doctor out there who doesn't recognise this feeling.

The case was investigated extensively by the hospital's adverse event investigation team. Even though this investigation took place recently, in a hospital with abundant expertise in incident analysis and a solid track record in patient safety education, the main recommendation that came out of the investigation addressed the paediatrician. A professional coaching programme should help him acquire an inquisitive attitude based on his own authority, instead of letting his conclusions be guided by other peoples' opinions. He should not have gone along so easily with his predecessors' suspicion of child abuse. This implies that if Dr Barth had had an adequately inquisitive attitude, he would not have missed the diagnosis and suspected the parents of child abuse. This implicit message was strengthened by the fact that the investigation report stated no further recommendations. No quality improvement recommendations for the Paediatric Department, none for the hospital as a whole. Just one recommendation, directed at a single doctor who, by the way, had never before been involved in a serious case of diagnostic delay or error. A dramatic event and the single most important lesson the hospital draws is that one doctor must go on a training course. It's a well-known reflex, also by the doctors themselves who are involved in diagnostic errors, to assume that personal failure is the root cause of the error. But is this really the most we can get out of cases of diagnostic error?

In 2003 I attended my first patient safety conference, in Halifax, Canada. It was an overwhelmingly inspirational conference for me. One of the presenters was Pat Croskerry, a big Canadian with snow-white hair and kind eyes, professor of emergency medicine at Dalhousie University in Halifax. He enthusiastically shared his first experiences with setting up patient safety training for medical students. His main theme was diagnostic reasoning, the way doctors arrive at their diagnoses. And how this can derail. Since then he has published an impressive amount of articles on this[1]. His work draws on the so called 'Dual Process Theory', established at the end of the 20th century by the American philosopher and psychologist William James. Others have further developed James' theory over the years. Amongst these is Daniel Kahneman, who was awarded the Nobel Prize in 2002 for integrating this theory into the economic sciences. His book *Thinking, Fast and Slow* is widely acclaimed[2]. Dual Process Theory is not the only theory about the way the human mind works, but it is broadly endorsed and has been tested using fMRI research[3]. In short, the theory boils down to humans having two different systems of thinking: intuitive and reasoning. The intuitive system, also called type 1 or associative, is used most often. It's fast, often subconscious, based on prior experience, generally correct but more prone to errors. The reasoning system, also called type 2 or analytical, is slow, costs a lot of energy but more often leads to correct conclusions. It's estimated that we use our intuitive system 95% of the time. The intuitive system is characterised by short-cuts, pattern recognition, rules-of-thumb and associative thinking. This is very functional, because it saves us a lot of time and energy in our daily life. It carries a danger in it, though: that we misinterpret the available information. When this misinterpretation happens systematically, it's called a bias; an inclination to hold on to a partial perspective, neglecting the possible merits of an alternative perspective. Biases are often subconscious. Over 100 different types of bias have been described. Some biases many people will recognise are:

- Anchoring bias: holding on to a conclusion despite information to the contrary.
- Availability bias: deeming one conclusion most likely because it is the first that came to mind.
- Attentional bias: basing your conclusions on an event or information that is more memorable.
- Bandwagon bias: drawing a conclusion because many others have drawn the same conclusion. This is also called 'groupthink'.
- Confirmation bias: looking for, interpreting and remembering only the information that confirms your conclusion.

These are just some examples starting with the first three letters of the alphabet. Countless publications and internet sites describe many, many more biases.

So there are over a hundred different ways a human can make a cognitive error. Doctors are humans and that makes them prone to these errors. Paediatrician Barth is not the only one to draw the wrong conclusion and make a diagnostic error. Doctors miss relevant diagnoses on a regular basis. In 2003 *JAMA* published a review article on diagnostic errors discovered at autopsy audits[4]. The researchers found that 23.5% of the diagnoses contained major errors, missed diagnoses related to the cause of death. Nearly one out of four. In 2015 the USA-based Institute of Medicine published its report, *Improving Diagnosis in Health Care*, warning that, "most people will experience at least one diagnostic error in their lifetime, sometimes with devastating consequences"[5]. It seems safe to assume that cognitive biases play a role in many of these diagnostic errors.

For people who regularly make decisions that have enormous impact, like doctors, it is important to be aware of the existence of cognitive biases. But it is even more important to know how to prevent biases luring you towards the wrong conclusion. One way to prevent this from happening is by deliberately switching from type 1 to type 2 thinking. Because type 2 uses a more analytical thinking process, the chances of being tricked by a bias are smaller. But using type 2 thinking for every decision is not feasible in real life, just like obtaining complete diagnostics for every patient isn't feasible. It costs too much time, effort and resources. There are more patients waiting out there to been seen. Besides, biases can also creep into type 2 thinking and the whole problem is that you're not aware of biases influencing your conclusions. 'An inquisitive attitude based on his own authority', as Dr Barth was recommended, wouldn't help either. Basing your conclusions on your own authority is precisely the behaviour that will set you up for biases such as confirmation and anchoring bias.

From daily life we know it is difficult but possible to recognise and mitigate prejudice, so it must also be possible in healthcare, to some extent. Much has been published on this so-called debiasing, but research is still in its infancy and far from conclusive. There have been some promising strategies that seem to have some effect, mostly in a simulated environment[6]. Croskerry describes three types of intervention that form a spectrum together: educational, workplace and forcing functions[7]. Education and training can help prevent biases in the future. This begins with understanding how humans think and the role biases can play[8]. After this phase, there are interventions we could use in daily practice, like guided reflection or a checklist of some sort[9]. An example of a guided reflection is inducing reflective reasoning by having the doctor write down the suspected diagnosis, list the findings that support this diagnosis, list the findings that speak against this diagnosis and list the findings that would be expected to be present if the diagnosis were true, but were not found. Then the doctor should list alternative diagnoses assuming that the initial diagnosis was incorrect, and to follow the same procedure for each alternative diagnosis. Finally, the doctor should draw a conclusion by ranking the diagnoses in order of likelihood and selecting the final diagnosis for the case. This was tested on internal medicine doctors by Sílvia Mamede and her research team. Her publication in *JAMA* suggested this method improved diagnostic accuracy[10]. When such methods are mandated, you arrive at the third type of intervention, the forcing function. The effectiveness of 'forcing' doctors to use checklists has been proven, for example in operating theatres and in reducing central line infections. Taken together, these interventions could help mitigate the effect of biases in diagnostic reasoning.

Let's return to Rachel's case and the question whether we could draw more lessons from this case than just the conclusion that training the paediatrician might help. It was Rachel's third emergency visit to the hospital in a relatively short time span. The symptoms Rachel presented (excruciating pain, neurological failure) were not in line with the trauma mechanism the father described (spontaneous fall, fallen from bed). She also had notable bruises, older and recent ones. When a child is presented with injuries not consistent with the explanation given for them, or notable bruises without an explanation, the cause unfortunately is more often physical abuse than a neurological disorder. This set the trap for availability bias. The doctors who had seen Rachel at her first hospital visit had made a subtle reference in her chart to child abuse as a possible cause. The second doctor had taken this one step further by already filling out the child abuse detection instrument as required by law in case of substantial suspicion and adding this to her chart. Because the suspicion at that time was substantial but not enough to intervene, he had left it at that. When Dr Barth saw Rachel at her third presentation in the hospital, her presentation was very much like the previous two times, strengthening the suspicion of abuse (confirmation bias). On top of that, Rachel's father acted strangely. He mainly spoke about himself instead of his daughter. His speech was a little slurred and he walked with a drunk man's gait. His shabby appearance and low education added to the impression of a man possibly not all that capable of taking care of children. This led to attentional bias distracting the doctor's attention from the patient's symptoms towards the patient's environment. This shower of biases washed away the weaker signals that contradicted abuse as a cause. This should not be held against Dr Barth, it could have happened to any of us.

But how can you prevent this happening to you? Guided reflections like Mamede used could help, but this can only act as a forcing function if it is used at all times, including those times when you feel confident about your diagnosis. Especially then. Personally, I feel it would be very difficult to implement a structural guided reflection when you are confident of your diagnosis. Firstly, because the doctor is often alone, there is no social control like there is for performing a time-out in an operating theatre. Secondly, because it costs time. But foremost because the doctor does not feel it is useful to do, because they feel confident that they have drawn the right conclusion.

Maybe a shorter version might work, only aimed at preventing biases luring you in the wrong direction: by always asking yourself, just before you draw a definitive conclusion, if there are any findings that speak against your conclusion. If so, switch to your analytical system to formulate for yourself why these findings give insufficient cause to reconsider your conclusion. This is a question you could also pose during meetings where patients' diagnoses and treatment options are discussed. So don't ask 'if' there are any contradictory findings, but 'which' findings are contradictory. By formulating it as an open question you activate the participants' analytical cognitive systems. "Which findings are not in line with the diagnosis, and why did you disregard these findings?" My advice is to make a note of the outcome of this discussion in the patient's chart, for two reasons. Firstly, because as time progresses more contradictory findings may pop up and then you can accumulate these instead of weighing them each separately (see Chapter 10). Secondly, so you can reconstruct how you came to your conclusion. This can be instructive should the diagnosis turn out to be wrong.

In Rachel's case one of the contradictory findings was the father's cerebellar condition. The story he kept telling about his ADCA (autosomal dominant cerebellar ataxia) was not picked up as a relevant finding. Harshly put, the doctors probably thought, "What is this strange man droning on about?" His slurred speech and the tangential way he told the story did not help increase the father's credibility. His behaviour felt like a distraction from the focus of the doctors' attention, the injured child. The father's talkative behaviour was seen as disruptive, and disruptive behaviour has been shown to impair doctors' diagnostic reasoning[11]. However, the father's story was in fact a signal that the child may suffer from a hereditary neurological condition. It turned out the father never had ADCA, but FHM, just like his daughter. This rare neurological condition caused the symptoms in both Rachel and her father.

Cognitive biases are inevitable pitfalls in human reasoning. Those who are aware of this are less surprised when it happens to them. As a doctor, you cannot escape making diagnostic errors now and then, sometimes with dramatic consequences. You can, however, improve your chances of catching diagnostic errors in time by consciously looking for findings that contradict, instead of supporting, your diagnosis.

HOW CAN THIS HELP ME TODAY?

Cognitive biases are tenacious and largely subconscious pitfalls in clinical reasoning. When you're on the verge of embarking on a care path with major consequences for the patient, force yourself first to answer this question:

- Which findings are not in line with my conclusion?

HOW CAN I INVOLVE MY PATIENTS?

When you're on the verge of embarking on a care path with major consequences for the patient (for example, a surgical procedure or a significant time span before the next doctor's appointment), explain to the patient on which grounds you have based your conclusion and ask if he/she feels you might have overlooked anything in your reasoning.

CHAPTER 14
Professional performance

THE CASE

In the end, this story has only losers. I've been racking my brain but cannot see what we should have done differently, if there could have been another way to handle the situation. Should we have intervened earlier, acted more resolutely? Or should we have done the opposite, given Fred more space, one more chance?

It was the end of the eighties when I joined my GP practice. Fred Hackett had been working there as a GP for some years already. We tend to be, if I may say so myself, quite a progressive practice. We were one of the first with an electronic patient record and a direct electronic line with the main pharmacies around. We always made room to accommodate GP registrars or students. Our practice consisted of four to seven GPs, it shifted a bit over the years due to differences in working hours. With most I had excellent relationships. Of course we sometimes had a colleague who was just not my type, but the group was large enough for this not to be a problem. I had always been fond of Fred. He was affectionate, funny and always prepared to take over your on-call shift if something came up. An ideal colleague and the type of GP I would want to go to myself. At least, that was how I felt all those years.

Maybe the first portent was the moment Fred told us he did not want to supervise registrars and medical students anymore. This was about 5 years ago. It remained unclear to me whether something had happened to prompt this. One day during our weekly meeting Fred, out of the blue, declared that he felt uncomfortable with the current generation of trainees. There was some kind of mismatch. He expressed how much he had always enjoyed supervising and that the time had come to hand this task over to the younger generation GPs in the practice. At the time we didn't think too much of it, it seemed a normal enough request. If he did not want to be a trainer anymore, that was fine. In the months following his request, we saw him less and less at the monthly educational meetings we organised. That was, I realise now in hindsight, a tell-tale sign that he was changing. I did not pay any attention to it at the time, I thought it was in line with Fred not supervising anymore.

Three years ago the first incident happened. Or maybe I should rephrase: the first we became aware of. Fred missed a myocardial infarct when he was on call. He had visited the patient at home after the patient's wife had called the emergency number. The patient's wife later recalled that Fred had hardly examined her husband and had reassured them that the symptoms were due to a gastric condition. He had given the patient antacids and left them with the advice to call the GP practice in the morning if the pain hadn't reacted enough to the medication. One hour later the patient's wife had called an ambulance and her husband was admitted to the local hospital while being resuscitated by the paramedics. She filed a complaint and we discussed the case extensively. To better understand the situation, I should tell you that missing a myocardial infarct is a classic mistake within primary care. If we referred everybody with chest pain to the hospital, our entire healthcare system would collapse. We try our best to distinguish between acute and non-acute causes of chest pain, but sometimes we get it wrong. So we could see how this could have happened to Fred. Even so, we did have some questions and one or two colleagues had a bad feeling about the incident. I must admit I was not one of them. I had, in hindsight maybe naively, accepted the explanation Fred gave us. He claimed he had performed a proper physical examination, contrary to what the patient's wife had said, and that it regularly happened that a patient or the patient's family had an incomplete recollection of events in these kind of situations. We should take into account that this was an uneducated couple, Fred added. And the way the patient had presented his complaints did not correspond with a cardiac cause. He had not complained about pain radiating to his jaw or upper arm and the chest pain had started right after a high-fat meal. In the end we concluded that there was a discrepancy between the account provided by the wife and the account Fred provided but that we had found insufficient indication of negligence or inadequate practice.

This incident left its mark on Fred, that much was clear. He became less outspoken within the group and seemed ill at ease around some of our colleagues. I noticed he increasingly skipped our group meetings and slowly retreated from activities not directly related to patient care. When I asked him about this, he answered with a smile that these activities had never been his cup of tea, they just distracted him from what healthcare should be about: taking care of patients. "Every hour I spend around a meeting table, is an hour lost to patient care." And in the same breath he would ask me how my children were doing or enthusiastically report on some new exhibition he had recently visited with his wife.

One day my colleague Nadia Fakhoury stepped into my room while I was doing my administration. She closed the door behind her, looked around uneasily and then said: "Bill, I don't know how to say this, but we are worried about Fred. We feel he's losing it, it's becoming serious." Nadia took a seat and told me how our youngest colleague, Eline Kielson, had come to Nadia a few weeks ago to voice her concern in confidence. She had seen a couple of Fred's patients when she had been on call. In her opinion these patients had been receiving inadequate care by Fred. She had given multiple examples, such as badly regulated diabetes, missed informed consent, delays in referral of patients and treatment that was not in line with national guidelines. Eline had tried to talk about this with Fred, but had experienced his reaction as unreceptive. He downplayed common examples, and met concrete examples with a defensive demeanour. He called it difference in interpretation, accused the diabetic patient of noncompliance with therapy and complained about ridiculous guidelines. Eline had hit a brick wall and so, with her heart in her shoes, had turned to Nadia for help. Because I was the oldest after Fred, Nadia came to me. "We have to do something about this situation, Bill. This just doesn't feel right anymore." A chill crept up my spine. How should I go about this, how do you start a such a conversation? Whichever way it went, the relationship between Fred and the rest of the colleagues would be damaged. My own relationship with Fred might suffer. And what if they were wrong? And what if they're right, how come I hadn't seen it myself? I scanned through Fred's patients I had seen out of hours and my own patients Fred had treated out of hours or in my absence. Yes, I had seen some irregularities. Antibiotics I would not have prescribed, a missed ankle fracture, stuff like that. Things that could happen to me too, I had thought at the time. Had I ever discussed these findings with Fred? Not that I could remember. And absolutely, Fred was Fred in his own typical way. Everybody has their mannerisms, I guess. No reason to split hairs… I did discuss a missed meningitis with him once. Fred had given a credible explanation and it had not occurred to me to bring this up in the group.

The conversation with Fred was the toughest conversation in my life. This was a whole other ballgame compared to breaking bad news to patients. Initially Fred tried to downplay the situation, it was all a little over the top. Then he suggested Eline was not cut out for the job. Then he appealed to our years of friendship. As the conversation progressed, it became increasingly unpleasant. It was all a conspiracy to get rid of him, him of all people, who had just 4 more years to go before retirement. It was lack of respect. He had built up this practice with his bare hands and now they wanted him out? "The last word has not been said about this," he roared and stormed out of the room.

From that moment on, Fred only communicated with us through his solicitor. The whole affair cost us a fortune and a ton of wasted time. It was distressing, it was downright ugly. In the end an independent external committee was appointed and scrutinised a series of Fred's patient charts and established that these had indeed shown substandard practice too often. There were even some cases of patients whose death was possibly related to substandard care. Eventually the legal battle ended. Fred stopped practising and moved shortly after. I never had the chance to talk to him after our awkward conversation. I lost a respected colleague and a friend. That hurt and still hurts. But what disturbs me most to this day is that I had been blind to his gradual downfall all those years.

Or, if I am totally honest, had missed the courage to face it.

REFLECTION

Every case of poor professional performance is a personal tragedy. For the patients who, often unknowingly, received inadequate care; for the professional him- or herself; and for the colleagues who could not or did not intervene.

Nobody signs up for something like this. Professional performance deficiencies seldom arise acutely. It's like a coronary artery slowly filling up with plaque due to an unhealthy diet. Portents of imminent heart failure are neglected until, one day, the stenosis blocks the artery and leads to acute hypoxia of the heart muscle. Even if treatment is on time and the heart survives, permanent damage has been done. Those who experience professional performance issues all agree with one thing: prevention is better than cure.

There are several different definitions for poor professional performance. I'll give you three to give some idea. The British Medical Act describes 'deficient professional performance' in section 35C as a standard of professional performance that is unacceptably low and which (save in exceptional circumstances) has been demonstrated in a fair sample of the doctor's work. It is seen as conceptually separate from negligence and from misconduct. The Medical Council of Ireland describes poor professional performance as a failure by the doctor to meet the standards of competence (whether in knowledge and skill, the application of knowledge and skill or both) that can be reasonably expected of doctors practising the type of medicine practised by the doctor[1]. The Royal Dutch Medical Association (KNMG) defines poor professional performance as a structural situation of irresponsible care in which the patient is harmed or runs the risk of harm and in which the professional is not (or no longer) able or prepared to solve the problem him- or herself[2]. All definitions refer to some kind of repetitive situation. Poor professional performance is more than a one-time mistake or lapse in quality. And almost always, the people around the professional involved are aware of the problems long before they become public.

In 2013, a consortium of Dutch research institutes published a report on poor professional performance[3]. They concluded that the factors contributing to poor professional performance can be sorted into three categories:

- Personal factors (e.g. fatigue, depression, burn-out, family issues, hubris).
- Work-related factors (e.g. isolated work, culture, inadequate leadership).
- Educational and developmental factors (e.g. safety issues not embedded in medical training, lack of professional standards).

The researchers state that it's almost always a combination of the individual and the setting he or she works in that leads to the development and/or protraction of performance issues. You could say it's an imbalance between strength and burden.

Healthcare professionals run a high risk of experiencing the personal factors described above at some point in their career, especially burn-out. Research on 2400 Dutch medical specialists revealed that 55% experienced a high amount of stress at work[4]. Research in 2009 on 2100 Dutch general practitioners showed that 21% met the clinical criteria of burn-out[5]. Another Dutch study claimed that 15% of doctors will at some time in their career be impaired in their professional responsibilities by alcohol, drugs or a mental illness[6]. Mexican researchers showed that burn-out symptoms have already arisen at medical school and develop progressively. Fourth to sixth year students showed moderate burn-out in 28% and severe burn-out in 8% of respondents[7]. An Indian study of 588 interns and residents showed that more than one-third had burn-out symptoms and that burn-out increased with the number of years of residency[8]. If you delve into this further, you will find many studies and publications on the high incidence of stress-related factors that can impede the quality of professional performance. Taken together, these suggest that burn-out is a significant problem among medical professionals from their early years on, and that the problem is pervasive on multiple continents and in multiple cultures. All things considered, it seems a miracle that actually so many healthcare professionals keep their performance up to par.

A large risk in the category 'work-related factors' is an isolated work environment. A former colleague of mine, Maarten de Wit, who handled many cases of poor professional performance at the Dutch Healthcare Inspectorate, described it to me once in cycling terms as 'dropping out of the peloton'. Somebody can't keep up or takes the wrong exit and a widening gap develops between this individual and the rest of the group. This was the case in nearly all of the high-profile cases of poor professional performance. The consultant who builds up his own group of patients that are never seen by colleagues, the GP who stops supervising registrars, the department that does not keep up with (inter)national developments and stagnates to a quality level that was sufficient in the 1980s but is now seriously outdated. This risk manifests itself from two sides: the individual (or group) that falls back and the environment that does not react to this.

When I was doing my medical training rotations at the end of the 1990s, I witnessed an example of an environment that did not react to an individual 'regressing from the mean'. It took place during my rotation in internal medicine. At the first handover meeting where I presented a patient, one of the consultants started sighing loudly. With both elbows on the table and his head in his hands. He just sat there, shook his head and sighed. You can imagine I became quite insecure. Had I said something to cause this reaction? I looked around to see how others were reacting. Nothing out of the ordinary, the rest were looking at me or at the papers that lay before them. Nobody seemed to pay any attention to the moaning consultant, it was as if I was the only one who noticed. So I pulled myself together and continued presenting my patient. Afterwards I spoke to one of the other junior doctors about this. She said: "Oh, just ignore it, that's just how Dr X is." This turned out to be right on, because during the following weeks he always acted like this at handover meetings. A week or so after my first encounter, I witnessed him on the ward. He was looking over the list of admitted patients in the nursing quarter. "Oh no, Mrs Y is here again. She's mad as a hatter, simply refuses to take her medication. Make her take her meds and get her out of here asap." The registrar stood beside him and looked perplexed. Awkwardly she told Dr X that he might be mistaken, as this was the first time Mrs Y had been admitted to the hospital. And so it went on. At the time I knew nothing about patient safety, and it did not occur to me that the situation could be detrimental to the patients. It did not cross my mind to speak up about it, either at the hospital or to one of my supervisors at the medical faculty. I took this to be normal. But I also felt that if it was indeed normal, I would never want to work in such an environment. Looking back after all those years, the memory fills me with sadness and a little anger too. It's deplorable that nobody at that hospital had the courage to protect Dr X from himself. Or protect the patients, because I cannot envision a scenario in which this kind of behaviour does not pose a risk for the quality of patient care. Maybe his colleagues did not see it anymore, because they had become used to his behaviour as it gradually progressed from slightly odd to maladjusted to unfit. They didn't know any better. "That's just how Dr X is."

The image of 'dropping out of the peloton' brings to mind many examples from outside the field of healthcare: financial institutions, housing associations, educational institutions whose directors had lost touch with reality and created a parallel universe in which the behaviour they had gradually accepted as permissible was clearly reprehensible in any normal civil society. The fallen leaders in Arabic nations also showed some telling examples of outrageous behaviour, such as gold plated Kalashnikovs, millions of dollars in walls and theft from state resources. The interesting thing is, the Romans already knew that we humans are not capable of handling absolute power. Consul of Rome was a position somebody held for a maximum of 1 year, and always together with somebody else so each could hold the other in check. I cannot reach any other conclusion than that all of us, myself included, are prone to derail if we spend significant time in an environment in which we are never contradicted or corrected. This not only holds true for the Consul of Rome, dictators and City bankers, but for everyone with professional autonomy.

Luckily many countries have adopted policies to help doctors keep their professional performance in line with professional and societal standards. In my own country, we have various forms of professional peer assessment focussed at the quality of care at department level or the quality of the juniors' training programme. Since 2008, hospitals have gradually, and sometime grudgingly, introduced systems to assess individual performance of doctors annually. The goal is to help doctors continuously improve their professional quality. We see that the younger generation is more at ease with this than the older generation who have practised for 10 or 20 years without anybody ever questioning the quality of their work. They see it as a threat or feel uncomfortable with the idea of another colleague giving them feedback, or with them having to give feedback to a colleague. And I can sympathise with that. It can be very uncomfortable, especially if there are issues to be confronted. But the alternative, having issues and not confronting them, can fester into situations far beyond 'uncomfortable'.

Everybody goes through times of suboptimal performance. Most often, it evens out naturally like a pendulum. If it drags on too long, and if you are not corrected or helped, you run the risk of becoming a 'poor performer'. Because this can happen to anybody, it should not be taboo to talk about it. Just like with vascular disease, we should feel free to talk about the risks so we can take preventive measures in time to prevent permanent damage. A healthier diet, stopping smoking, more physical exercise and medication if necessary. Speaking for myself, I am certain that I am prone to derail if I drop out of the peloton. So I encourage people to disagree with me and I organise feedback on my performance at regular intervals. I do this out of self-interest, purely for my own good. For example, I always ask my colleagues who are present for feedback after I conduct a conversation with a hospital board or medical professional in my function as inspector. These are often difficult and sometimes intense conversations, as comes with the territory of being a regulator. So afterwards I ask my colleague how he or she felt that I had done and what I could do better next time. I always ask, no matter what our hierarchical relationship is. The first reaction is often positive, "you did well". But then I keep asking. "Thanks, but is there anything you feel I could have done differently? Did I miss any cues, could my message have come across more effectively?" Mostly my colleagues can come up with improvement suggestions if I try hard enough to pry it out of them. And yes, this can feel uncomfortable for both of us, but I really want to know. I sometimes have to suppress my knee-jerk reflex to react defensively, and force myself to hear them out. Out of respect for my colleague, but, again, primarily out of self-interest. And yes, I feel a bit disappointed in myself when they bring something up I could have done better. But you get used to it. And it feels good at some level. Certainly when I succeed in improving the issue they mentioned and tell them later on how their feedback helped me change. These are the little nudges that keep me close to the peloton. It doesn't always feel nice, but it beats waking up one day and realising you've become a Fred Hackett.

HOW CAN THIS HELP ME TODAY?

Everybody goes through times of suboptimal performance. Without some form of correction, this situation can progress into poor professional performance. Mobilise your environment to regularly give you honest feedback on your performance.

HOW CAN I INVOLVE MY PATIENTS?

Use the outcome of patient satisfaction surveys in your self-assessment. Ask patients with whom the doctor–patient relationship has come to an end to tell you how they've experienced you as a doctor and what you could improve for future patients. Explain, if necessary, that patients often feel awkward in giving a doctor candid feedback, but that you need their feedback to improve and continuously remain sufficiently patient-focussed.

CHAPTER 15
Open disclosure

THE CASE

Three years ago our daughter Nicky fell off her horse during a show jumping competition and broke her back. If I close my eyes I can still see her fall in slow motion. There's a lot I could tell about all the things that happened afterwards, but the most important thing is that Nicky recovered almost completely. You can't imagine how relieved we were. She underwent spinal surgery to repair the broken vertebrae and stabilise the spine. After a period of rehabilitation, Nicky went back to university on time for the start of the new term. Unfortunately the pain in her back never completely disappeared and her study results declined somewhat in her second year. We returned to the trauma surgeon with her complaints, but he could find no specific cause for the pain. He saw nothing unexpected or abnormal on the X-ray of her spine. The neurologist could not find any cause for her complaints either, even after a thorough physical examination. Nicky kept her cool and concluded she would just have to learn to live with this pain. She was grateful she wasn't stuck in a wheelchair. Her resilience has always been so unbelievably impressive.

When Nicky returned home after spending 2 months in Central America to help restore a school building, we noticed her condition had deteriorated. She also seemed to have a bit of a limp now. It took me some effort, but eventually she consented to a hospital visit. She was seen by a neurologist who, after examining her, referred her to a physiotherapist. There seemed to be no neurological explanation for her condition. Without complaining once, Nicky saw a physiotherapist for the following 3 months. I did not see any significant improvement, but this was not something I discussed with Nicky.

At Christmas we got a terrible scare. Nicky called to me from her bedroom. She wasn't able to get out of bed. Her legs felt numb and she couldn't move them. My husband called an ambulance and our daughter was sped to the hospital. We literally waited for hours in the emergency room before a neurologist came to see us. Dr Enfield was dressed like a gentleman, but a bit quick with his conclusion.

He asked Nicky to walk some steps in the hallway. Fortunately Nicky's condition had improved enough by then for her to be able to walk again. He hit Nicky on her knees with his little hammer, performed some other quick physical tests and then came to sit with us.

"I cannot find any neurological disorder." He shifted uneasily in his seat. "I think your daughter might have what we call conversion disorder. This is basically a condition in which a patient shows psychological stress in physical ways. This may be due to her riding accident, subconscious frustration about the consequences, stress. This can result in physical symptoms. As neurologist I am not suited to treat her for this. I can, however, recommend an excellent psychiatrist. Here, I will write down his name for you on a card."

I was baffled. What utter nonsense. Had I not seen with my own eyes that Nicky had been paralysed this morning? Nicky of all people had never been a pretender, had never overly complained about any illness she had had. My husband and I exchanged glances, we both looked at our daughter who was still sitting on the examination table. I was so dumbstruck that Dr Enfield had placed the card in my hand and had left before I fully realised what had happened. I dropped the card in the waste bin without even looking at what he had written on it. We collected our stuff and left the hospital. Nicky made a new appointment with her physiotherapist.

Four months later it happened again. All of a sudden Nicky lost control of and sensitivity in her legs. We called an ambulance again, but now we persuaded the paramedics to drive us to a different hospital.

Here Nicky was seen by a neurologist and a rehabilitation specialist at the same time. They seemed very alarmed by her story and by the results of their physical examinations.

"To break it to you, we are afraid you might be developing paraplegia," they told Nicky. "We're going to order an emergency CT scan and let you know as soon as we have the results." The scan showed that one of the bolts that had been used to stabilise the spine had dislodged and moved into the spinal canal, causing pressure on the spinal cord. Nicky underwent emergency surgery to remove the bolt. The trauma surgeon who had operated on her in the other hospital after her accident came by to visit Nicky 2 days after the operation. He apologised sincerely that he had not seen that the bolt had dislodged. He had taken the X-rays with him that were made when he had examined Nicky's complaints. He showed us how, in hindsight, we could see the bolt was displaced slightly at that time already, penetrating into the spinal canal. He was so sorry he had overlooked this and that Nicky had now had to undergo emergency surgery. It genuinely upset him. We almost felt more sorry for him than for our daughter. Three weeks after surgery, Nicky was transferred to a rehabilitation clinic.

Our experience with neurologist Enfield last December bothered us. Of course the dislodged bolt had caused her symptoms at that time too. Not stress or subconscious feelings. We spoke about this and all three of us felt we needed some form of closure in relation to this event. We wanted to speak to him about it. To tell him the outcome and to express our discontent. I took it on myself to plan the meeting. Well, that did not go quite as we had anticipated…

It took me no fewer than four telephone calls to arrange an appointment. The man seemed to have quite the agenda. We were already seated when he stepped into the room. He flipped through Nicky's patient chart.

"Hmm, peculiar story. Oh well, I'm glad you're feeling better now." He hardly looked at Nicky. "And how can I be of service at this moment?"

We tried to explain that we had felt he had not taken Nicky's complaints seriously and had hardly performed any diagnostics to find the possible cause. But we didn't seem to get through to him. It felt like there was a wall around him preventing any form of rapport between us. Dr Enfield was evasive and tried to impress with medical jargon. He shifted in his chair, pinched his moustache and repeatedly took off his glasses to polish them with his handkerchief. This neurologist clearly did not intend to make an apology of any sorts. It did not seem to occur to him that he had made a mistake, that he had failed Nicky. We were exasperated. And then, just like at Christmas, Dr Enfield suddenly left the room, leaving us behind in disbelief. At that point I became furious. First he lets us down, and now he insults us with his arrogance. This was unacceptable. We contacted a solicitor, sued Dr Enfield for negligence and reported the case to the regulator.

REFLECTION

In the previous chapters, I have tried to share the knowledge on patient safety that I was fortunate enough to acquire over the past 15 years. My hope is that this can help you reduce the chance of becoming involved in a serious adverse event yourself. However, despite your best efforts, it can still happen to you. In this chapter I will propose ways of dealing with such a situation. Specifically, how the healthcare professionals involved can prevent further emotional harm for the patient, or the patient's family, in the wake of an adverse event.

There is an abundance of recent literature on the subject of 'open disclosure': being open and forthright with the patient or family after an adverse event. The first document I read about this theme was the 2006 Harvard Consensus Report called *When things go wrong: responding to adverse events*[1]. The goal of this report was "to stimulate clinicians and hospitals to develop their own clear, informed, explicit, and effective policies for managing and preventing, where possible, the ongoing pain that [adverse events] engender". The report considers three aspects: 1) dealing with the patient and family; 2) dealing with the caregivers; 3) managing the event. With regard to dealing with patient and family, the main goal is to repair the relationship. For this, the authors say, it is necessary to:

- Be open and honest.
- Apologise.
- Explain what will be done to prevent future adverse events.

Dr Enfield did not succeed in repairing the relationship, he did not even seem to try. Engaging in an open and honest dialogue after an adverse event can be extremely difficult for the healthcare professional involved. Paediatrician and neonatologist Harry Molendijk, one of the founders of the patient safety movement in the Netherlands, said it was "like breaking bad news, only now you are part of the bad news". Healthcare professionals are expected to be calm and professional and display empathy and rapport with the patient, while these same healthcare professionals are at that very moment overwhelmed by their own emotions: guilt, shame, self-criticism, anger, fear of the consequences for the patient, fear of the consequences for themselves and their colleagues, grief, just to name a few. "I wished I could just curl up and hide behind a stone," one doctor once summarised his feelings to me. And within this turmoil of emotions, you are expected to be open, calm and empathetic. The degree to which a caregiver is capable of this feat depends on factors such as aptitude, upbringing, training and the circumstances of the moment. HALT from Chapter 8 is certainly of influence. If you are tired or under time pressure, this dialogue will be a bigger challenge than if you are well rested and without other pressing appointments. In other words, multiple factors influence the degree to which you will be able to engage adequately in this type of dialogue. Not even the most seasoned healthcare professional will be immune to feelings of insecurity after being involved in an adverse event. And if he or she is immune, that would be all the more reason to support this person during the interaction with the patient or family, because the chances are he or she will come across as unsympathetic. This is neither in the interest of the patient, nor in that of the caregiver. Therefore, it is always wise to ask for help, to organise support before engaging with the patient or family after an adverse event. To protect you from your own vulnerability at that moment. In the interests of both the patient and yourself.

In 2010, the USA-based Institute for Healthcare Improvement (IHI) published the report *Respectful Management of Serious Clinical Adverse Events*[2]. The lead author is Jim Conway, who was Chief Operating Officer at Dana-Farber Cancer Institute at the time of two high profile adverse event in the 1990s. One of these concerned a well-known journalist who died due to a chemotherapy overdose. This led to a 3-year period of intense media coverage and scrutiny by regulatory authorities. But it also led to an important momentum to learn and improve patient safety. Some of these lessons concerned dealing respectfully with patients or the bereaved. By 2010 the IHI regularly received urgent requests from organisations seeking help in the aftermath of serious adverse events. Who must do what, and when? The reports says: "The risks of not responding to these adverse events in a timely and effective manner are significant, and include loss of trust, absence of healing, no learning and improvement, the sending of mixed messages about what is really important to the organization, increased likelihood of regulatory action or lawsuits, and challenges by the media". The report is mainly written for the board and management of healthcare organisations, to help them manage the process after an adverse event. One of the elements that need managing is support for the healthcare professional in engaging with the patient or family. The authors stress the importance of timely, open and honest communication. And they add: "Research demonstrates that disclosure of adverse events is often associated with higher ratings of quality by patients and a drop in malpractice suits"[3].

Also in 2010, the insurance companies in the Netherlands joined forces and published a guideline for managing the aftermath of an adverse event, called GOMA[4]. Ground breaking in this guideline was the emphasis insurers laid on the importance of being open about mistakes. Till then, the popular belief among Dutch physicians was that insurance companies forbade them to admit any errors they made because that would lead to malpractice claims. Recommendation 8 from the GOMA guideline states: "If investigation of the event leads to the conclusion that a mistake has been made, then the healthcare provider admits this mistake and apologises to the patient". In the commentary later on in the guideline, the authors write: "In the event of a mistake, it is recommended not to avoid or mask the word mistake. This can lead to tension in the dialogue the patient can easily place. Patients tend to have very well tuned bullshit sensors. We recommend you apologise and explain what is being done to prevent the occurrence of similar adverse events in the future".

I want to pause a moment to note that it is not wise to admit a mistake before you're certain a mistake has actually been made. Not only out of self-interest, but also in the interest of the patient. When I worked at the University Medical Centre Utrecht, a young patient suddenly and unexpectedly died during a procedure. The specifics of the situation made the doctors infer that the procedure was the cause of death and thus that a mistake must have been made during the procedure. Wanting to be open and honest, this was communicated with the parents right after telling them their child had died. Several weeks later, the committee that had thoroughly investigated this dramatic event came to the conclusion that the cause of death was most likely not the procedure, but an underlying medical condition. This new insight was very difficult to sell to the parents. It came across as though we were covering up, hiding the truth. This caused a lot of unrest that could have been prevented if the premature conclusions, drawn in the heat of the moment, had not been shared with the parents. It's better not to talk about 'mistakes' as long as the causality of events is unclear. This does not mean I promote defensive behaviour. On the contrary. You can always say you're sorry, even if the causality of events is unclear. "I am very sorry this has happened to you" or "that this has happened" is an adequate first reaction after any unforeseen adverse outcome.

The legislation around adverse events differs between countries. Some countries, such as New Zealand, have so called 'no fault compensation' for medical injuries. This means the patient is not dependent on finding a healthcare provider at fault to be compensated for unintended harm. I advise you to find out what the rules are in your own country. But however they may be, and in whatever culture you work, it seems to always be the right thing to express empathy with the patient or family and to do your utmost to repair the relationship between the patient and the healthcare provider. The patient needs to be informed, but also needs to be heard. This last aspect, listening to the patient, is less well worked out in the publications I mentioned above.

In 2014, I was privileged to chair a full day mini-course at the International Forum on Quality and Safety in Healthcare. One of the presenters was Professor Rick Iedema, whom I had known for some years. A sympathetic and, to my opinion, very wise man, Rick is Professor in Healthcare Innovation at the University of Tasmania, and Research Manager at the Agency for Clinical Innovation of the New South Wales Ministry of Health, both in Australia. Rick has published many papers and reports on disclosure after adverse events in healthcare[5,6]. In the period 2009–2011 he was involved in the '100 patients' stories project' in which 100 patients were interviewed about what they would want if they experienced an adverse event[7]. Besides the aspects already mentioned earlier (apology, openness, honesty, explanation, safety measures to prevent recurrence) one new aspect came to light: patients wanted to tell their side of the story. They wanted to be heard. Disclosure, they felt, should be a two-way street, a shared dialogue. Patients wanted the opportunity to tell the healthcare professionals involved how they had experienced the events and what the consequences for them had been. They were disappointed they were not given this opportunity, that a true dialogue was not possible. At the same Forum session, one of the other presenters was Carolyn Canfield from Canada. Carolyn's husband, Nick, had tragically died in 2008 as a result of inadequate postoperative care. This experience turned Carolyn into an energetic patient safety champion. Since then she has led seminars and workshops to teach patient engagement for improving safety and has been a keynote speaker at safety conferences around the globe. At the Forum session, she argued that 'patient safety' is a notion constructed from the perspective of the healthcare provider, while the notion of 'harm' is fundamentally based on the patient's perspective. This leads to friction. Something can be 'safe' but still cause 'harm'. It can, for example, be safe not to let the patient's spouse accompany him to the operating theatre, but harmful to the couple to be forcibly separated in this time of need. Our definition of 'adverse event' neglects a large quantity of patients' experiences. Carolyn advocated that patient safety lessons should be reaped from multiple sources, not just those the healthcare providers deem relevant. This chimes with Professor Rick Iedema's findings. Carolyn went on to say that *primum no nocere*, first do no harm, sounded to her like a mantra for a malpractice insurance company, not as a moral compass for a caregiver. Healthcare is not about not harming people, it's about the relationship of trust between the patient and the caregiver, she proffered. Carolyn had looked through religious literature and suggested an alternative guiding principle for healthcare providers: 'I shall not forsake thee'. I will not abandon you.

Nicky and her parents felt abandoned by Dr Enfield. First during the emergency visit at Christmas, and anew when they tried to engage in a dialogue about what had happened. They had found the courage to initiate the dialogue in an attempt to repair the relationship, repair their trust in this doctor and maybe even in the healthcare system as a whole. To their disbelief, they met a wall of silence. This confirmed to them that the neurologist, to whom they had entrusted the care for their most precious one, did not care about Nicky and did not take the family seriously. Not even after it had become abundantly clear he had misjudged her symptoms, nearly causing paraplegia. This felt like insult upon injury.

Especially when something goes wrong, the guiding principle of 'I shall not forsake thee' is of utmost importance. It lays the groundwork for both the patient or family and the healthcare professionals to come to terms with what has happened. Don't abandon your patient. Not physically, by not showing up anymore, but also not emotionally, by shutting them out. No matter how difficult this might be for you at that moment. Because it is exactly that emotional abandonment that feels like betrayal to the patient or family, and can leave a scar far uglier than any physical injury could.

HOW CAN THIS HELP ME TODAY?

- Get to know the adverse event procedure of the healthcare organisation you work at, before you are confronted with an adverse event.
- Find out who can support you in case of an adverse event.

What should I do if I'm involved in an adverse event?

- Never abandon your patient.
- First contain the harm, if possible, to prevent further injuries to the patient.
- Delegate all your other tasks as soon as possible, so you can focus.
- Make sure you are directly supported by people who have experience handling adverse events.
- Be open and honest to the patient or family about what you know, and apologise. Try not to have this conversation alone, because you can be influenced by your own emotions.
- In follow-up conversations, make sure you don't only tell what you know, but also invite the patient or family to share their experience, thoughts and feelings. Create a shared dialogue.
- Follow the adverse event guideline of your organisation.

CHAPTER 16
Epilogue

Even if all the recommendations from this book were strictly adhered to by all healthcare professionals, healthcare would still remain inherently risky due to ingrained complexity and the human fallibility of its professionals. In this, healthcare is not alone. "The only way to make commercial aviation 100% safe, is by keeping the planes on the ground," Job Brüggen, safety manager of the Dutch Air Traffic Control, once told me.

This book is about situations where things go wrong. Far, far more often, things go right. That is why I want to end on a positive note. The past 10 years have brought impressive improvements to healthcare quality and safety. Some examples from my own country:

- Between 2007–2009 and 2010–2012 the mortality after cancer surgery dropped by 25%[1].
- The 30-day mortality after acute myocardial infarction dropped by 44% between 2000 and 2010[2].
- A similar decrease was seen for 30-day mortality after stroke[2].
- Hospital mortality decreased by 25% between 2005 and 2010, whilst overall mortality decreased by only 12% in the same period[3].

Many other countries have shown similar improvements. People working in healthcare around the world perform miracles every single day. This fills me with enormous admiration and I am extremely grateful to them. And when they are unintentionally involved in an adverse event, we should not fix the blame, but fix the problem. Whenever I consider how far we have already come in improving the quality of healthcare, I am filled with hope and excitement about how much more we can achieve.

I hope this book can help the reader contribute to the impressive improvements we are accomplishing in healthcare together.

CHAPTER 17
Summary

Through this book I want to share the knowledge and experiences I have been fortunate enough to collect over the past 15 years and offer healthcare professionals concrete suggestions on how they can avoid adverse events. Using real-life case stories of adverse events, I describe behaviour that impairs patient safety. The healthcare professionals involved were mostly not aware of this unsafe behaviour or the consequences this behaviour could have. In the reflection on each case I try to understand the behaviour and suggest alternatives that can help the reader improve patient safety. The 'lessons' from the book can be summarised as follows:

OUTSMART YOUR OWN FALLIBILITY

- Make sure that recognising crucial information is not solely dependent on your vigilance (Ch 2).
- Hungry, Angry, Late, Tired? → HALT (Ch 8)!
- Be aware that cognitive biases influence your reasoning (Ch 13).

DON'T LET YOURSELF BE TRICKED BY THE CIRCUMSTANCES

- Always keep the 'worst case scenario' in mind (Ch 1).
- Assume things have not been taken care of until proven otherwise (Ch 3).
- Keep searching if a referred patient seems less ill than expected (Ch 6).
- Never reassure a patient until you are sufficiently sure this is justified (Ch 6).
- Recognise the signs that can warn you of an impending adverse outcome (Ch 7).
- The course of the disease is a film, not a photo (Ch 9).
- Don't weigh a patient's risks factors separately, but add them up (Ch 10).
- Make your own assessment of your patient's condition (Ch 12).

USE YOUR ENVIRONMENT

- Communicate the most likely scenarios (Ch 4).
- Organise regular feedback on your performance (Ch 14).
- Engage the patient in improving the safety of his or her care (all chapters).

KEEP IN MIND THAT NOBODY WANTS AN ADVERSE EVENT

- Speak up if you have a safety concern (Ch 5).
- Do not judge people on outcome, but on their behaviour (Ch 11).
- Don't ignore signs of poor professional performance (Ch 14).

REMAIN THE CAREGIVER

- Never abandon your patient, especially after something goes wrong (Ch 15).

References

INTRODUCTION

1 Langelaan M, Bruijne MC de, Broekens MA, *et al.* Monitor Zorggerelateerde Schade 2011/2012. Dossieronderzoek in Nederlandse ziekenhuizen. Nivel EMGO+/VUmc. Utrecht. 2013.
2 Leistikow I, Mulder S, Vesseur J, Robben P. Learning from incidents in healthcare: the journey, not the arrival, matters. *BMJ Qual Saf* 2016 Apr 1. pii: bmjqs-2015-004853. doi: 10.1136/bmjqs-2015-004853. [Epub ahead of print]
3 Carayon P, Schoofs Hundt A, Karsh BT, *et al.* Work system design for patient safety: the SEIPS model. *Qual Saf Health Care* 2006;**15**(Suppl 1):i50–8. Review.
4 Vincent C. Reporting and learning systems. In: Vincent C (ed). *Patient Safety*, 2nd edn. Chichester: Wiley Blackwell, 2010, 75–95.
5 Mitchell I, Schuster A, Smith K, Pronovost P, Wu A. Patient safety reporting: a qualitative study of thoughts and perceptions of experts 15 years after 'To Err is Human'. *BMJ Qual Saf* 2015 Jul 27. pii: bmjqs-2015-004405. doi: 10.1136/bmjqs-2015-004405. [Epub ahead of print]
6 Macrae C. The problem with incident reporting. *BMJ Qual Saf* 2015 Sep 7. pii: bmjqs-2015-004732. doi: 10.1136/bmjqs-2015-004732. [Epub ahead of print]
7 Kohn KT, Corrigan JM, Donaldson MS. *To Err is Human: Building a Safer Health System*. Washington, DC: National Academy Press, 1999.

CHAPTER 1

1 Dekker S. *Field Guide to Human Error Investigations*. Hampshire: Ashgate Publishing, 2006.
2 Blendon RJ, DesRoches CM, Brodie M, *et al.* Views of practicing physicians and the public on medical errors. *N Engl J Med* 2002;**347**(24):1933–40.
3 Haynes AB, Weiser TG, Berry WR, *et al.* A surgical safety checklist to reduce morbidity and mortality in a global population. *N Engl J Med* 2009;**360**(5):491–9.

4 De Vries EN, Prins HA, Crolla RMPH, *et al*. Effect of a comprehensive surgical safety system on patient outcomes. *N Engl J Med* 2010;**363**(20):1928–37.
5 Pronovost P, Needham D, Berenholtz S, *et al*. An intervention to decrease catheter-related bloodstream infections in the ICU. *N Engl J Med* 2006;**355**:2725–32.

CHAPTER 2

1 Institute for Safe Medication Practice https://www.ismp.org/tools/confuseddrugnames.pdf
2 Arimura J, Poole RL, Jeng M, *et al*. Neonatal heparin overdose – a multidisciplinary team approach to medication error prevention. *J Pediatr Pharmacol Ther* 2008;**13**(2):96–8.

CHAPTER 3

1 Reason J. Beyond the organisational accident: the need for 'error wisdom' on the frontline. *Qual Saf Health Care* 2004;**13**(Suppl 2):ii28–33.

CHAPTER 4

1 Gawande A. *The Checklist Manifesto: How to Get Things Right*. New York: Metropolitan Books, 2009.
2 Haerkens MH, Kox M, Lemson J, Houterman S, van der Hoeven JG, Pickkers P. Crew resource management in the Intensive Care Unit: a prospective 3-year cohort study. *Acta Anaesthesiol Scand* 2015;**59**(10):1319–29.

CHAPTER 5

1 ICAO Circular 153-AN/56, pp. 22–68.

CHAPTER 6

1 Weick KE, Sutcliff KM. *Managing the Unexpected: Assuring High Performance in an Age of Complexity*. San Francisco, CA: Jossey-Bass, 2001.

CHAPTER 8

1 Rogers AE, Hwang WT, Scott LD, Aiken LH, Dinges DF. The working hours of hospital staff nurses and patient safety. *Health Affairs* 2004;**23**(4):202–12.
2 The Joint Commission. Sentinel Event Alert 48. Health care workers fatigue and patient safety. 14 December 2011.

3 Landrigan CP, Rothschild JM, Cronin JW, *et al.* Effect of reducing interns' work hours on serious medical errors in intensive care units. *N Engl J Med* 2004;**351**(18):1838–48.
4 Nederlandse Vereniging voor Heelkunde. Normering Chirurgische Behandelingen 4.1. June 2014.
5 WHO patient safety curriculum guide: multi-professional edition. 2011.

CHAPTER 9

1 Endsley MR. A taxonomy of situation awareness errors. In: Fuller R, Johnston N, McDonald N (eds). *Human Factors in Aviation Operations.* Aldershot, UK: Ashgate, 1995, pp. 287–92.
2 Siu J, Maran N, Paterson-Brown S. Observation of behavioural markers of non-technical skills in the operating room and their relationship to intra-operative incidents. *Surgeon* 2016;**14**(3):119–28.
3 Singh H, Davis Giardina T, Petersen LA, *et al.* Exploring situational awareness in diagnostic errors in primary care. *BMJ Qual Saf* 2012;**21**(1):30–8.
4 Berwick DM. What 'patient-centered' should mean: confessions of an extremist. *Health Affairs* 2009;**28**(4):555–65.

CHAPTER 10

1 Achieving situational awareness in five minutes. The rule of three. Energy Institute, Hearts and Minds. November 2006.
2 Tibballs J, Kinney S, Duke T, *et al.* Reduction of paediatric in-patient cardiac arrest and death with a medical emergency team: preliminary results. *Arch Dis Child* 2005;**90**:1148–52.

CHAPTER 11

1 Leape LL. Testimony, United States Congress, House Committee on Veterans' Affairs; 1997 Oct 12.
2 Reason J. *Managing the Risks of Organizational Accidents.* Hampshire: Ashgate Publishing Limited, 1997.
3 Heringa MP, Leistikow IP. Open over fouten. Voorspelbaar, respectvol en transparant omgaan met incidenten. *Medisch Contact* 2008;**63**:1226–9.
4 Marx D. *Whack-a-Mole: The Price We Pay For Expecting Perfection.* Dallas: By Your Side Studio, 2009.
5 Dekker S. *Just Culture. Balancing Safety and Accountability.* Hampshire: Ashgate Publishing, 2007.

Recommended reading

http://sidneydekker.com/just-culture/
http://www.safetyandjustice.nl/

CHAPTER 12

1 Hollnagel E. *The ETTO Principle: efficiency-thoroughness trade-off: why things that go right sometimes go wrong.* Aldershot: Ashgate, 2009.
2 Vaughan D. *The Challenger Launch Decision: risky technology, culture, and deviance at NASA.* Chicago: University of Chicago Press, 1996.

CHAPTER 13

1 Croskerry P, Singhal G, Mamede S. Cognitive debiasing 1: origins of bias and theory of debiasing. *BMJ Qual Saf* 2013;**22**(Suppl 2):ii58–ii64.
2 Kahneman D. *Thinking, Fast and Slow.* New York: Farrar, Straus and Giroux, 2011.
3 Croskerry P. Clinical cognition and diagnostic error: applications of a dual process model of reasoning. *Adv in Health Sci Educ* 2009;**14**:27–35.
4 Shojania KG, Burton EC, McDonald KM, Goldman L. Changes in rates of autopsy-detected diagnostic errors over time: a systematic review. *JAMA* 2003;**289**(21):2849–56.
5 Balogh EP, Miller BT, Ball JR. *Improving Diagnosis in Health Care.* Washington: National Academy of Sciences, 2015.
6 Graber ML, Kissam S, Payne VL. Cognitive interventions to reduce diagnostic error: a narrative review. *BMJ Qual Saf* 2012;**21**(7):535–57.
7 Croskerry P, Singhal G, Mamede S. Cognitive debiasing 2: impediments to and strategies for change. *BMJ Qual Saf* 2013;**22**(Suppl 2):ii65–ii72.
8 Reilly JB, Ogdie AR, Von Feldt JM, Myers JS. Teaching about how doctors think: a longitudinal curriculum in cognitive bias and diagnostic error for residents. *BMJ Qual Saf* 2013;**22**(12):1044–50.
9 Lambe KA, O'Reilly G, Kelly BD, Curristan S. Dual-process cognitive interventions to enhance diagnostic reasoning: a systematic review. *BMJ Qual Saf* 2016 Feb 12. pii: bmjqs-2015-004417. doi: 10.1136/bmjqs-2015-004417. [Epub ahead of print]
10 Mamede S, van Gog T, van den Berge K, *et al.* Effect of availability bias and reflective reasoning on diagnostic accuracy among internal medicine residents. *JAMA* 2010;**304**(11):1198–203.
11 Mamede S, Van Gog T, Schuit SC, *et al.* Why patients' disruptive behaviours impair diagnostic reasoning: a randomised experiment. *BMJ Qual Saf* 2016 Mar 7. pii: bmjqs-2015-005065. doi: 10.1136/bmjqs-2015-005065. [Epub ahead of print]

CHAPTER 14

1 https://www.medicalcouncil.ie/Public-Information/Making-a-Complaint-/Glossary-of-Terms.html
2 KNMG Kwaliteitskader medische zorg, Koninklijke Nederlandsche Maatschappij tot bevordering der Geneeskunst, April 2012.

3 Wagner C, Lombarts K, Mistiaen P, *et al.* Onderzoek naar de aard en omvang van de problematiek van disfunctionerende beroepsbeoefenaren in de Nederlandse gezondheidszorg. Nivel, 2013.

4 Visser MRM, Smets EMA, Oort FJ, Haes HCJM de. Stress, satisfaction and burnout among Dutch medical specialists. *CMAJ* 2003;**168**(3):271–5.

5 Prins JT, van der Heijden FM, Hoekstra-Weebers JE, *et al.* Burnout, engagement and resident physicians' self-reported errors. *Psychol Health, Med* 2009;**14**(6):654–66.

6 Mook WNKA van, Gorter SL, Kieboom W, *et al.* Poor professionalism identified through investigation of unsolicited healthcare complaints. *Postgrad Med J* 2012;**88**:443–50.

7 Asencio-López L, Almaraz-Celis GD, Carrillo Maciel V, *et al.* Burnout syndrome in first to sixth-year medical students at a private university in the north of Mexico: descriptive cross-sectional study. *Medwave* 2016;**16**(3):e6432. doi: 10.5867/medwave.2016. 03.6432.

8 Ratnakaran B, Prabhakaran A, Karunakaran V. Prevalence of burnout and its correlates among residents in a tertiary medical center in Kerala, India: A cross-sectional study. *J Postgrad Med* 2016;**62**(3):157–61.

CHAPTER 15

1 When Things Go Wrong: Responding to Adverse Events. A Consensus Statement of the Harvard Hospitals. Burlington, MA: Massachusetts Coalition for the Prevention of Medical Errors, March 2006.

2 Conway J, Federico F, Stewart K, Campbell M. *Respectful Management of Serious Clinical Adverse Events.* IHI Innovation Series white paper. Cambridge, MA: Institute for Healthcare Improvement, 2010. (Available on www.IHI.org)

3 Kachalia L, Kaufman S, Boothman R, *et al.* Liability claims and costs before and after implementation of a medical error disclosure program. *Ann Intern Med* 2010;**153**:213–21.

4 Openheid medische incidenten; betere afwikkeling Medische Aansprakelijkheid (goma). De letselschaderaad, 2010.

5 Iedema R, Allen S. Anatomy of an incident disclosure: the importance of dialogue. *Jt Comm J Qual Patient Saf* 2012;**38**:435–42.

6 Birks Y, Entwistle V, Harrison R, Bosanquet K, Watt I, Iedema R. Being open about unanticipated problems in health care: the challenges of uncertainties. *J Health Serv Res Policy* 2015;**20**(Suppl 1):54–60.

7 Iedema R, Allen S, Britton K, *et al.* Patients' and family members' views on how clinicians enact and how they should enact incident disclosure: the '100 patient stories' qualitative study. *BMJ* 2011;**343**:d4423.

CHAPTER 16

1 Integraal Kankercentrum Nederland. Operatiesterfte na kankerchirurgie sterk gedaald. 16 oktober 2013. (www.iknl.nl)
2 Rijksinstituut voor Volksgezondheid en milieu. Zorgbalans. Versie 3.8, 26 September 2013.
3 Ploemacher J, Israëls AZ, van der Laan DJ, *et al.* Gestandaardiseerde ziekenhuissterfte daalt in de tijd. *Ned Tijdschr Geneeskd* 2013;**157**:A5267.

Index